Indian Instant Pot® Cookbook

Indian
INSTANT
POT®
COOKBOOK

**Traditional
Indian Dishes
Made Easy & Fast**

Urvashi Pitre

**ROCKRIDGE
PRESS**

The garam masala recipe originally appeared in *660 Curries* by Raghavan Iyer (Workman Publishing, 2008). It is reprinted with permission.

For general information on our other products and services or to obtain technical support, please contact our Customer Care Department within the United States at (866) 744-2665, or outside the United States at (510) 253-0500.

Rockridge Press publishes its books in a variety of electronic and print formats. Some content that appears in print may not be available in electronic books, and vice versa.

Photography © Melina Hammer, cover, pp. ii, xii, 8, 11 & 55; Hélène Dujardin, p. vi; Alan Richardson/Stockfood, p. x; Artography/Shutterstock.com, p. 8 (moong dal); René Riis/Gräfe & Unzer Verlag/Stockfood, p. 22; Eising Studio - Food Photo & Video/Stockfood, p. 33; Babett Lupaneszku/Stocksy, p. 40 & back cover; Darren Muir/Stocksy, p. 66; Jeff Wasserman/Stocksy, p. 79; Clive Streeter/Stockfood, p. 90; Jonathan Gregson/Stockfood, p. 105; Joerg Lehmann/Stockfood, p. 122; Renée Comet/Stockfood, p. 140.

Author photo © John Kasinger

ISBN: Print 978-1-93975-454-7
eBook 978-1-93975-455-4

To my family, who puts up with all the not-so-perfect recipes, and to my readers, who trust me enough to make my recipes for their families.

Contents

Namaste

I love to cook and to share recipes. Which is odd, because I'm terrible at following recipes, and I'm especially bad at following Indian recipes. They often contain an intimidating list of ingredients and multiple steps, and by the time I'm done reading them, I'd just as soon eat a peanut butter sandwich.

EASY AND AUTHENTIC

I want to show you how you can easily and authentically replicate the recipes I grew up making, without resorting to jarred sauces and premade pastes. I understand that not everyone has easy access to a variety of exotic ingredients. This book uses the most basic ingredients that are needed to create the delicious flavors of Indian cooking. I've included a visual primer on the eight spices and the eight dals that you will need to cook these recipes. Over time you may want to add to your repertoire, but this is a good start.

TRIED AND TESTED

Every recipe in this book has been tested, not just by me but by several generous people in the Instant Pot® Community Facebook group as well as by readers of my blog, TwoSleevers.com. Everyone excitedly reported back the pros and cons of what they learned, and I used many of those recommendations to further refine and streamline the recipes. Make each recipe once as written and then feel free to experiment. In fact, the book has suggestions throughout on how to improvise—how, for instance, Butter Chicken (page 98) can easily turn into other dishes. Many testers doubled, tripled, and even quadrupled the recipes with good results, and kept cooking times the same.

Namaste to you and yours, and thank you for letting me guide you to becoming an accomplished cook of Indian cuisine.

CHAPTER 1

Indian Food, Easy & Fast

I began cooking for my family and for myself when I was 14 years old. I was expected to prepare dinner for the family every evening, and because of my mother's generous heart, "family" meant anyone who happened to be staying with us or strolling by the house at dinnertime.

I didn't find any delight in cooking. I resented working in the kitchen while my friends got to enjoy being teenagers. But my mother worked, which was unusual in those days, so the cooking fell to me. Also unusual was the fact that my parents grew up in different parts of India—my mother in Punjab, up north, and my father in Maharashtra, in the west not far from coastal Bombay (now known as Mumbai). The different foods, and food traditions, associated with the two locations meant that I learned to cook a wide range of dishes native to many parts of the country.

No matter that I would complain about doing those household chores; my mother demanded that I learn to run a household. She wanted me to have the skills that I would need to live an Indian life. It wasn't until much later, after moving to America, marrying my first husband, and raising my own children, that I started to use my cooking knowledge. I was surprised to discover that many people had never learned how to cook. I thanked my mother silently for ensuring that I was equipped for life on my own, and for developing my ability to cook for my family.

Yet as my career took off, I found there were not enough hours in the day to get everything done, especially for a newly single mother of two boys. I found myself reaching for convenience foods a little too often. One night, the doorbell rang. "Pizza!" my little son excitedly exclaimed. How often had that doorbell rung with pizza on the other side? I knew it was time to bring homemade food back into our home.

I was determined but overwhelmed before my husband Roger came into the picture. He took one look at my disorganized kitchen, sighed, and went to work. A technical geek, he made sure everything was in its place and accessible. He shopped for all the tools we needed and planned time for us to be in the kitchen. With these changes, I found myself looking forward to cooking, and thinking that it could even be fun.

FROM MY KITCHEN TO YOURS

It's no secret that Indian food relies heavily on the use of spices for flavoring. Do we really need all those spices and ingredients to cook Indian food? I say no. This book is about capturing the traditional flavors of Indian cooking using simpler, less laborious methods than I was taught to use as a girl.

While creating the recipes for this book, I spent hours considering how to streamline the steps. Could I substitute garam masala in place of a handful of whole spices? What might I eliminate that didn't have a material impact on the final flavor? I dedicated myself to testing, and retesting, recipes until I felt I had captured an authentic taste and the recipe could be prepared in under an hour. A trained scientist, I essentially used scientific methodology to control different aspects of my experiments until I had reliable, repeatable recipes.

The result of these efforts is this book, a collection of Indian recipes that have been tried and tested. These recipes work efficiently and reliably to produce meals you will be proud to serve to your family and friends. But just because these rich and complex dishes can be created quickly doesn't mean they look like they were made quickly. The recipes in this book will also impress all those whom you (effortlessly) prepared them for.

THE PRESSURE COOKING TRADITION

The stove top pressure cooker has long been used in Indian cooking. When the pressure is released at the end of cooking and the steam pours out, the device makes a whistle-like sound, similar to a steam train's whistle. Over the years, the sound of the pressure-cooker whistle became the harbinger of mealtimes. When you heard that shrill noise, you knew the bustle in the kitchen was coming to an end and that the call to mealtime would soon follow. Everyone would gather together over the meal, and the talking, laughter, and sharing of stories would begin. The Instant Pot® brings to this rich heritage the ease that comes with self-regulation, making the whistle a relic of the past. When the meal finishes cooking now, it's a melodic beep that reminds us that dinner is at hand and it's time for everyone to come to the table.

In India's hot, tropical climate, all-day cooking is not a pleasant experience. Pressure cookers are especially appreciated for their quick cooking that reduces heat buildup in the house. This is why, even though our home has air-conditioning, I still use my Instant Pot® to bake cakes in the middle of a Texas summer.

Pressure cooking is important technology for Indian cooking for many reasons.

TIME. As the Indian diet largely relies on plant proteins such as legumes and beans for sustenance, pressure cooking is the fastest way to cook them—think 15 to 30 minutes versus 1 to 2 hours.

RESULTS. Pressure cooking results in a much creamier texture than is possible by stove top cooking.

FLAVOR. When you cook meat with a large quantity of spices, pressure cooking helps infuse the meat with additional flavor. Many Indian meat dishes are cooked in sauces containing complex flavors and blends of spices. The pressure cooker allows these flavors to meld together quickly, and the resulting meal tastes like it was cooked for hours.

TENDERIZING. Pressure cooking does an excellent job of breaking down and tenderizing tougher cuts of meat, allowing for the purchase of less expensive meat and, at the same time, making it possible to prepare melt-in-your-mouth weeknight dinners.

One Family, Two Food Histories

Just as people differ in dialects and food preferences from one part of the United States to another, so it is for the states of India. Mostly a source of humor (and occasional irritation) for relatives and friends, the different food traditions of my family differ as much as would the cuisines from Maine and Louisiana.

PUNJAB

My mother was from the Indian state of Punjab. Punjabi cooking relies on rich onion and tomato masalas, and on the liberal use of ghee, cream, and dairy products. Punjab is known as the bread basket of India because of its ample production of rice and grains.

Most of the food served in Indian restaurants in the United States is Punjabi food. Classically popular Punjabi dishes and foods include:

- Butter chicken
- Rajma (red kidney beans)
- Chana masala
- Palak paneer
- Naan

Punjabis are known for their hospitality and their generosity in sharing food. As a result, anyone who happened to be in, or sometimes simply near, our house at mealtime would be invited to sit down with our family.

MAHARASHTRA

My father is from the Indian state of Maharashtra. For flavor, the food relies on coconut, jaggery (a type of unrefined sugar), peanuts, white sugar, and cilantro. These ingredients are widely available in Maharashtra, and the cuisine uses them to enhance, but not overpower, the flavors of vegetables and legumes. Unlike Punjabi dishes, Maharashtrian dishes are almost never served outside of India, so there is far less familiarity with them internationally. This cookbook includes popular (but relatively unknown) dishes such as masalé bhat, matki, and shrikhand.

Maharashtrians are known for being—how can I put this diplomatically?—somewhat less generous when it comes to their sharing of food. While Punjabis will give you half of everything they have in the house (which presents an entirely different etiquette challenge for the recipient), you're more likely to be told by a Maharashtrian, "We're about to have lunch. Can you please come back later?" This is quite a standing joke among Maharashtrians themselves, who are well aware of their reputation. This contrast has led to some uncomfortable times in our household.

My mother's horror at turning away a dinnertime guest was matched only by my paternal grandmother's horror at having strangers join us for dinner. I love my Maharashtrian side, but I think I am more Punjabi in this respect, so if you come to my house at mealtime, expect to be fed.

EASE. Pot-in-pot cooking allows you to cook rice at the same time as the main dish, knocking out with one appliance half of what you're expected to make for an Indian meal. With the addition of a cooked vegetable, some chapatis, and perhaps a fresh chutney, the traditional Indian dinner is ready.

INSTANT LOVE

Before the Instant Pot® became an indispensable appliance in my kitchen, I naturally had a stove top pressure cooker. And I thought it was just fine. But as far as I'm concerned, the Instant Pot® is far superior to a stove top pressure cooker.

IT IS VERSATILE. It's a rice cooker, a yogurt maker, a slow cooker, and, with the release of the Ultra model, even a sous vide device. It allows you more strict control over cooking temperatures than a stove top pressure cooker, with settings like Soup that keep liquids from coming to a rolling boil. My chicken curry with yogurt uses the Soup function to keep yogurt from separating, which allows for a smooth, tangy, hearty sauce.

IT REQUIRES NO BABYSITTING. The most valuable asset for me—and for many a harried parent—is the ability to put food in the appliance and to walk away and allow it to do its job. Traditional pressure cookers require monitoring time under pressure carefully, controlling the heat, and so forth. The Instant Pot® does all that for you. When your children are acting fractious, when you and your partner need some time together, or when a friend needs to talk with you on the phone, it's wonderful to know that dinner is cooking. What a great way to feed both body and soul!

IT HAS SEVERAL SAFETY FEATURES BUILT IN. Did you know that if you burn something at the bottom of your pot, it won't come to pressure? That if the pressure becomes too high, it has an internal safety mechanism that activates, shifting the inner pot downward to create a gap between the lid and the inner pot? Steam is released from the gap into the internal chamber, and the heating is stopped. These are only 2 of the 10 or more safety features that have been built into this marvelous device.

IT'S HELPFUL FOR THOSE WITH MOBILITY ISSUES. If you or someone you love has issues with mobility, as I occasionally do because of my

Rethinking the "Instant" in Instant Pot®

I have made every attempt to list reasonable prep and cooking times for the recipes in this book, but bear in mind that the total time for a recipe also includes the time it takes for your pot to come to pressure, as well as to release pressure. How long it takes for the pot to come to pressure is controlled by how full your pot is and how many servings you're making. Even if a recipe says it cooks in 15 minutes under pressure, please allow yourself 30 to 45 minutes for the entire process the first time you make it.

Which brings us to the notion of "instant." Certainly, some things cook faster in the Instant Pot® than they do by other cooking methods. Red meats and dry beans are classic examples of foods that cook in less than half the time that they do on the stove. While kidney beans and chickpeas take 1 to 2 hours on a stove top, they take only 20 minutes at pressure in an Instant Pot®.

But this is not true of more delicate foods such as fish, vegetables, and some cuts of chicken. These foods may take as long to cook in the pressure cooker as they do on the stove top. So why use the Instant Pot®? I find it useful even in those circumstances for four main reasons:

1. **One-pot cooking.** Dishes such as biryani that are notorious for requiring multiple steps and dirtying every pot in your kitchen can be cooked in one appliance. Thanks to the stainless steel inner pot, cleanup is a breeze.

2. **Hands-off cooking.** There is no need to watch the fish and test it repeatedly to prevent overcooking, and no need to stir constantly to keep the milk from burning as you make your paneer.

3. **Better flavor.** Cooking under pressure infuses the food with flavor in a way stove top cooking can't match. When I try the same recipe on the stove top and in an Instant Pot®, the difference is remarkable. Remember, your meat is not boiled under pressure, it's superheated. This results in a very different taste profile.

4. **Heat efficiency.** Not leaving your oven on for hours, not heating up your house, and not having smells permeate throughout your house can be a wonderful thing. I love being able to steam fish, like I did for the Patra ni Macchi (page 92), and not have the house smell of fish for days.

So while it might not always be faster, the Instant Pot® has other advantages in terms of flavor and efficiency.

FRENCH LENTILS

MOONG DAL

CINNAMON

CHANA DAL

CARDAMOM

TURMERIC

CAYENNE

CLOVES

rheumatoid arthritis, the Instant Pot®, with its ability to produce delicious meals without a need for constant interaction, will prove to be a godsend. On days when I am in pain or tired, it is easier, faster, and more nourishing to cook at home with my electric pressure cooker than it is to order out. With the right recipe and ingredients, you can put dinner on the table faster than having food delivered to your door. Not to mention that cooking at home saves you a lot of money.

THE INDIAN PANTRY

There are many books and resources that can give you the history and origin of every spice you might use in Indian cooking. My intention is to reduce the investment you make in spices but still allow you to have everything you need in your pantry. Most cooks will have salt, pepper, and cooking oil. Many will have bay leaves and basmati rice. Beyond that, however, you do not need an entire arsenal of spices and ingredients before you can start cooking. The most affordable place to get pantry items is at a local Indian grocery store. If you don't have one close by, there are many options for purchasing online.

Spices

Spices are at the heart of Indian cooking, and they are crucial to the flavor of our food. With a few exceptions (which I'll point out), I recommend that you buy whole spices. Spices begin losing flavor the moment they are ground. It takes only a few minutes, or less, to grind them, and the immediate aroma of the freshly ground spices is almost payback enough for the effort. You can pay $6 or $8 for a minuscule jar of ground spices that has already lost much of its flavor, or you can buy a pound of whole seeds at an Indian grocery store for the same $6 or $8. The seeds will last long after the spice in the jar hardens, and if you don't grind them until a year later, they will still be as fresh as the day you bought them. All that freshness translates directly into flavor.

All seed spices can be used in dishes in at least four ways: added as whole seeds, ground into powder, roasted and then ground, or fried to infuse their flavor into ghee or oil. Each of the methods imparts a different flavor profile of the spice into the food. Using whole spices will let you enhance and expand your repertoire of spice blends. For the recipes in this book, you will need the following spices. Each should be purchased whole, unless otherwise specified.

- Cardamom pods
- Cayenne pepper (ground)
- Cinnamon
- Cloves

- Coriander
- Cumin
- Peppercorns
- Turmeric (ground)

Dals and Beans

Dals, or lentils, are essential to Indian cooking. In a country that's largely vegetarian, the notion of combining rice and beans, or rice and dals, to create a complete vegetarian protein is second nature. Our reliance on plant proteins over the centuries has ensured that we always have either rice or wheat breads with our meals.

As you get into Indian cooking, you will realize that the ubiquitous term "dals" is meaningless to an Indian. Just as the Inuit have 50 words to describe snow, Indians have a myriad of foods loosely classified as dals, including moong, masoor, urad, tuvar (each of these in whole or split form), kidney beans, chickpeas (white, black, or green)—there's a whole new culinary world awaiting your discovery.

If you don't have an Indian grocery store near you, you might find these dals at the bulk bins at specialty grocery stores, where you can buy as much or as little as you want. If you buy just 1 cup of each, it will cost you a few dollars, and you'll be able to cook them and see which ones you like. For the recipes in this book, you will need the following dals and beans:

- Chana dal
- Chickpeas
- French lentils
- Masoor dal

- Moong dal
- Rajma kidney beans
- Split moong dal
- Whole urad dal

MASOOR DAL

PEPPERCORNS

WHOLE URAD DAL

CUMIN

RAJMA KIDNEY BEANS

CORIANDER

SPLIT MOONG DAL

CHICKPEAS

Herbs

Two herbs are used more often than any others in Indian cooking: fresh cilantro and fresh mint. Luckily they're both readily available outside of India. While mint is used to flavor and season, cilantro is used to flavor as well as garnish. If you are among the 10 percent of the population who are genetically predisposed to find that cilantro tastes soapy, don't worry about it. Either substitute parsley or leave it out altogether. None of these dishes rely solely on cilantro for their main flavor.

Packaged, Bottled, Canned

The recipes in this book rely largely on fresh products and homemade spice mixes. Nonetheless, there are a few staples you will want to have on hand.

BASMATI RICE. Look for aged Indian basmati, grown in India. Despite extensive taste testing, I have not found American-grown basmati to be anything but an extremely distant cousin to the real thing.

CANNED TOMATOES, DICED. Pressure cooking fresh tomatoes can sometimes yield unpredictable results. Depending on their moisture content, fresh tomatoes can either cook well or burn. To produce reliable results with these recipes, I used canned tomatoes.

COCONUT MILK, FULL-FAT. While we often make our own coconut milk in India, I find canned full-fat coconut milk—especially the brands with no additives—a perfectly fine substitute.

RAISINS. Golden raisins are often used in desserts such as rice kheer, as well as in chutneys. Having these in your pantry will make last-minute cooking a lot easier.

SAFFRON. Despite its expense, saffron is a spice I use a bit of for special occasions. Nothing comes close to the fragrance and taste that just a few threads can impart.

SHREDDED COCONUT, UNSWEETENED. I often use this instead of fresh coconut, which doesn't last as long and is a lot harder to find. The pressure cooker, with its high heat and moist environment, reconstitutes these shreds in no time. Do not use the sweetened shreds used for baking—they will significantly alter the taste of the final dish.

ESSENTIAL EQUIPMENT

Wouldn't it be nice if the Instant Pot® were the only piece of kitchen equipment we needed? While it is multifunctional, it can't do it all. Here are some other tools that will come in handy.

COFFEE GRINDER. A coffee grinder or spice grinder (which is at its heart the same product branded in two different ways) is essential for

Instant Pot® Terminology

I don't use abbreviations in this book, but I do on my blog, and if you read websites or belong to online discussion groups dedicated to the Instant Pot®, you'll find that, like many groups, they seem to have their own language. Here are a few of the common terms and abbreviations you may see:

IP: Instant Pot®

Natural pressure release (NPR or NR): Letting the pressure inside the pot drop on its own

Pot-in-pot (PIP) cooking: Cooking ingredients in a bowl or baking dish placed on a trivet inside the pot

Quick release (QR): Moving the pressure-release valve to release the steam all at once

Sling: A strip of aluminum foil used to remove a bowl from the Instant Pot®

Trivet: A metal or silicone rack (usually with handles) on which food is placed for steaming

freshly ground spice mixes. The 5 minutes it takes to make your own blends will more than pay off in the flavors you are able to produce with them. If possible, set aside one grinder just for spices and grind your coffee in a different one. Otherwise, run a slice of bread through it after grinding spices to completely remove the powders, and use the seasoned bread crumbs in creative ways.

BLENDER OR FOOD PROCESSOR. To make these recipes easier and better suited for the Instant Pot®, I often ask you to use a blender or food processor to finely purée aromatics such as ginger, garlic, onion, and even tomatoes. Blending not only ensures a smooth final product and extracts every bit of flavor from the aromatics, it also allows them to caramelize slightly in the Instant Pot® and prevents you from having to add water to cook the recipes.

IMMERSION BLENDER. Indian cooking does not rely on cornstarch for thickening. While we do sometimes use besan (chickpea flour) for thickening, most of the thickness comes from either the vegetables or the dals used in cooking. I call for an immersion blender for the Butter Chicken (page 98), as well as for several dal recipes. While you could use a regular blender, putting hot liquids into a blender comes with a few risks—not to mention producing one additional container to clean. A reliable immersion blender will earn its keep in providing you with thick, creamy sauces and dals.

FINE-MESH STRAINER. A strainer is useful for straining your chai, and if large enough, it can also do double duty for straining Greek yogurt.

STAINLESS STEEL CONTAINERS WITH SILICONE LIDS. When the recipe calls for pot-in-pot cooking, I prefer using stackable stainless steel bowls or containers. Not only does steel conduct heat better and ensure faster cooking than other types of metal, it is also safe, and it cleans up easily. Your local Indian grocery store can show you their selection of "pressure cooker dabbas," as can an internet search. While the silicone lids are not entirely necessary, they are heat-resistant, waterproof, and reusable. I prefer them to covering my containers with foil, but if you don't have any, you can certainly cover with foil and get good results.

SILICONE MITTS. These mitts are ideal for removing hot items from the pot. Traditional oven mitts absorb water, which makes using them to remove hot items from a pressure cooker a little tricky. These inexpensive items make cooking in an Instant Pot® a little safer.

FREQUENTLY ASKED QUESTIONS

I often post Instant Pot® recipes on my blog, and I always get lots of comments and feedback, which I love. While many people quickly master a few recipes, many wish to do even more with the appliance. Even though it's my priority to create easy, simple recipes, I still want those recipes to help you explore and enjoy your appliance, as well as expand your palate. Here is a collection of some of the questions I get asked most often, and my answers to help you on your journey as you cook Indian food in the Instant Pot®.

Can't I just buy the garam masala? Won't any garam masala do?

Yes, you can certainly buy the garam masala, but no, not any garam masala will do. For a while there was an avid debate between people who had made and loved my Butter Chicken (page 98) recipe and those who found it bland. The ones who loved it could not believe that anyone could've found this flavorful dish bland!

The difference was entirely in the garam masala. When I asked people to show me pictures of which garam masala they used, we learned that some brands sold a blend that was almost exclusively paprika! No wonder it couldn't replicate the flavors in cinnamon, cayenne pepper, chile, cloves, cumin, and coriander.

I urge you to buy whole spices, as they are versatile and long-lasting. But if you prefer not to do that, please look over the garam masala recipe in this book and try to find a garam masala that uses all or many of the same spices. Otherwise, you may be making a Hungarian goulash rather than Indian butter chicken!

When should I use natural release versus quick release?

Many of the recipes call for a combination of both. I prefer to use natural release for 10 minutes and then quick-release the remaining pressure. There are two situations where I use quick release.

› Many vegetables and seafoods such as fish or shrimp require a short cooking time. Allowing them a natural release results in an over-cooked dish.

› Quick release is often used when you plan to add items to a dish halfway through cooking. This style of cooking in stages can be quite useful when making, for example, the Pork Saag (page 116), where you cook the meat for a lot longer than the greens. In this case, you release pressure quickly after cooking the meat, add the greens, and then release pressure quickly at the end to avoid overcooking.

Can I double the recipe, and if so, do I need to add more time?

You can certainly vary the serving sizes for any of these recipes without increasing the cooking time—cooking time under pressure, that is. But the fuller your pot, the longer it will take to come to pressure. Once under pressure, however, four chicken thighs will cook as quickly as eight thighs. So allow longer total cooking times, but increase the cooking time under pressure by only a minute or two—at most.

How much liquid do I need for every recipe?

We've all been told that the Instant Pot® needs at least 1 cup of liquid before it can come to pressure. Yet many of the recipes in this book call for no added water. How is that possible?

You do need water for the Instant Pot® to come to pressure. But I prefer to get that water from the meat and vegetables directly. Most meats and vegetables tend to release a lot of water as they cook. This flavorful broth seasons the dish better than tap water can. It also keeps you from having to boil away the excess water at the end, which can result in an overcooked dish. Pressure cooking imparts a better taste because it keeps your meat from being boiled as it cooks. Using the Sauté function to boil excess water defeats that purpose.

Note, however, that rice, beans, lentils, and other legumes do require water to cook. They absorb water and swell (and foam) as they cook. Use the amounts specified in these recipes and in pressure-cooking charts for the best results.

How full can I fill the pot? To the MAX line?

This is a commonly asked question, with an answer that is just as commonly ignored. Your inner cooking pot should not be more than two-thirds full of liquids or meats. If you're cooking foods that foam, such as beans or pasta, it should not be more than half full.

The only time when it is acceptable to have anything that is over the full line in your Instant Pot® is when you are doing pot-in-pot cooking, and it is the inserted pot that exceeds the line. Placing a pot over a trivet to make the steamed yogurt custard is one such instance. The pot contains only 2 cups of water, but the pot containing the custard may be taller than the full line.

This is an important safety consideration that should be heeded. Not only will the Instant Pot® shut itself off if you overfill, thus delaying your dinner, you also definitely do not want the contents to overheat and boil over.

Can I substitute proteins in the recipes?

It's very easy to customize many of the dishes by using the animal protein of your choice. Different meats have varying amounts of connective tissue and fat, which means that they cook at different rates. Substituting one for another is usually possible—it just requires a shorter or longer cooking time.

The chart below shows recommended times for meats. To substitute paneer or vegetables, make the sauce separately in the Instant Pot® and add paneer or vegetables to the cooked sauce. Then you can cook on Sauté until the ingredients are heated through or the vegetables are tender.

MAIN RECIPE	SUBSTITUTE	TIME UNDER PRESSURE *All times assume high pressure
PORK SAAG	Beef Saag	15 to 20 minutes, beef chuck cubes
	Chicken Saag	8 to 10 minutes, boneless chicken thighs
	Lamb Saag	20 minutes, lamb shoulder cubes
CHICKEN KORMA	Beef Korma	15 to 20 minutes, beef chuck cubes
	Lamb Korma	20 minutes, lamb shoulder cubes
BEEF CURRY	Chicken Curry	8 to 10 minutes, boneless chicken thighs
	Lamb Curry	15 to 20 minutes, lamb shoulder cubes
	Pork Curry	20 minutes, pork shoulder cubes

My sealing ring smells like garam masala. How can I get rid of the odor?

Hmmm . . . why would you want to? Okay, I'm teasing. While I love garam masala, it may not be the best thing to flavor your yogurt with.

A few things work to keep the sealing ring from retaining odors:

> Remove and wash it each time. But don't forget to put it back before cooking again!

> Prop the lid on the side of the pot to allow both pot and lid to air out.

- › Run a vinegar-water steam cycle in your pressure cooker for 10 minutes.

- › Set the sealing ring out in the sunshine to dry.

- › Soak the ring in denture cleaner (how do I know this, you wonder?).

- › Dedicate one ring for making sweets and another for preparing savory dishes.

Note, however, that just because your ring smells of something doesn't mean your food will taste of it. Personally, I use one ring to cook them all, and I haven't noticed any transfer of flavors (and yes, I totally used Sauron's line [from *The Lord of the Rings*] there).

Pressure Cooking at High Altitude

The higher the altitude, the lower the atmospheric pressure. This means that for cooking, the higher the altitude, the lower the boiling point of water (and other liquids) and the faster the water evaporates. When you get above an altitude of 2,000 feet, this can be significant.

While the sealed interior of a pressure cooker helps make up for the lower atmospheric pressure, you'll still have to make some adjustments if you live in the mountains and if you have any model of the Instant Pot® other than the Ultra. Most pressure cooker manufacturers recommend increasing cooking times by 5 percent for every 1,000 feet above 2,000 feet (so a dish that cooks under pressure for 20 minutes at sea level would cook for 21 minutes at 3,000 feet or for 22 minutes at 4,000 feet). Some manufacturers also recommend slightly increasing the amount of liquid.

If you have the Instant Pot® Ultra, there's no need to adjust cooking times. Rather, this model allows you to adjust the cooking settings up to 9,900 feet, and the machine will adjust cooking times accordingly.

THIS BOOK'S RECIPES

This book includes nearly 50 Instant Pot® recipes that primarily make use of the pressure cooker functionality, along with a couple of recipes for yogurt. In the chapter on kitchen staples, some recipes are made in the Instant Pot® and others (such as the spice mixes and chutneys) are not.

I tested (and retested!) all the Instant Pot® recipes in a 6-quart Duo and a 6-quart Ultra. Each model has its own nuances, so I've tried to keep the instructions as generic as possible. But here is a bit of info specific to different models that should be useful:

FOR THE DUO PLUS: Choose Pressure Cook whenever the recipe calls for the Manual setting. To adjust the heat level in the sauté function, after selecting Sauté, press the Sauté button again to toggle from low to medium to high heat.

FOR THE ULTRA: Use the dial to select Pressure Cook whenever the recipe calls for the Manual setting. To adjust the heat level in the sauté function, use the dial to select Sauté, then again use the dial to select the proper heat level (low, medium, or high).

FOR THE LUX: This model only cooks on high pressure. Whenever a recipe calls for cooking on low pressure, you may need to experiment to find the correct cooking time under high pressure. Start by subtracting 1 minute from the cooking time, and adjust from there.

Of course, time is always a factor when you decide to use your Instant Pot®. The recipes using the Instant Pot® break down for you the time required for every step (prep, sautéing, pressure cooking, pressure release), which the total time takes into consideration. Keep these time-related particularities in mind:

> All of my recipes assume about 10 minutes for the pot to come to pressure. The total time noted on recipes that pressure-cook factors 10 minutes for coming to pressure.

> Many recipes call for releasing pressure naturally, which tends to take anywhere from 10 to 15 minutes. The total time noted on recipes that call for natural release assumes 15 minutes for the pressure release.

> ‣ Several recipes call for releasing pressure quickly, which typically takes a minute or less. The total time noted on recipes that call for quick-release does not factor any time for the pressure release.

While these recipes could not be more hands-off, you must factor in some time beyond the time it takes to cook at pressure. The majority of recipes can be made, start to finish, in 45 minutes or less. A number of others will take 60 minutes or less. For Indian cooking, it doesn't get any faster!

Many people love naturally meatless Indian dishes. Wherever there is a vegetarian or vegan recipe in the book, you'll see a corresponding label.

Finally, I think we can all agree that some of our favorite recipes to make (if not to eat) require little more than adding the ingredients to the pot, starting cooking, and walking away. I call these "pour and cook" recipes. Each time there is one of these in the book, you'll see a "pour and cook" label so that you know your effort will be truly minimal.

LET'S DO IT!

Now it's time to start cooking. You know everything you need to know to cook delicious Indian meals in your Instant Pot®, and to produce food in your own kitchen that will rival what you can get in Indian restaurants. If you can chop, mix, blend, stir, and press buttons, you can make these recipes. None of them call for complicated techniques. Children as young as 10 years old have made many of these recipes with success. Children under two years old have eaten these with great enjoyment—as pictures I'm sent of sweet little faces smeared with butter chicken often remind me.

Remember that you know your family's tastes better than I do, so if you know they will hate a particular ingredient (hello, cilantro!), or that the ingredient might be too spicy for them (good-bye, cayenne!), change it up to personalize the dish.

Finally, keep in mind that when you make these recipes, you will not only have better-tasting, more authentic, more nutritious food at home, you will also be saving a lot of money. I once calculated the cost difference between making six Indian dishes at home versus ordering them from a restaurant—and the savings were enough to justify buying another Instant Pot®! If you're looking for a reason to become a two-pot household, now you have it. You're welcome.

Let's cook!

CHAPTER 2

Kitchen Staples

Garam Masala

VEGAN

PREP TIME: 5 minutes

This garam masala recipe was created by one of my favorite Indian recipe creators, Raghavan Iyer, author of *660 Curries*. I've tried many other recipes, and none have come close to this one, both for ease of making and for superior taste. I urge you to spend the 5 minutes it takes to make this mix. I've made liberal use of this garam masala across many recipes in this cookbook. Creating the mix at home will not only improve the flavors in your food, it will also help ensure your cooking tastes exactly like what I cook in my own kitchen. **MAKES ½ CUP**

2 tablespoons coriander seeds

1 teaspoon cumin seeds

½ teaspoon whole cloves

½ teaspoon cardamom seeds, from green or white pods

2 bay leaves

½ teaspoon ground cayenne pepper or ½ teaspoon red pepper flakes or 3 dried red chiles

1 cinnamon stick, broken up

1. In a clean coffee or spice grinder, add all the ingredients.

2. Grind until the spices form a medium-fine powder. Stop the grinder several times and shake it so all the seeds and bits get under the blades and grind evenly.

3. When you're finished, unplug the grinder. Holding the lid in place, turn the spice grinder upside down and shake the spice mixture into the lid. Pour the garam masala into a small jar with a tight-fitting lid. Store in a cool, dry place for up to 4 weeks.

Punjabi Garam Masala

VEGAN

PREP TIME: 5 minutes

COOK TIME: 3 minutes

This masala's distinct flavor comes from toasting the spices before grinding them. When you uncap this homemade spice mixture you will revel in its rich bouquet, which more than justifies the effort.

MAKES ¼ CUP

1 tablespoon coriander seeds

1 teaspoon cumin seeds

1 teaspoon whole cloves

½ teaspoon black peppercorns

3 cinnamon sticks, broken up

3 bay leaves, broken up

1. Place a small skillet over medium heat and add all the ingredients. Toast them until they're fragrant but not browned, 2 to 3 minutes. They will continue to cook for a while after you take them out of the pan, so if you're in doubt, undercook them.

2. Transfer the spices to a plate or a paper towel to cool.

3. Once cool, place the spices in a coffee or spice grinder. Grind until the spices form a medium-fine powder. Stop the grinder several times and shake it so all the spices get under the blades and grind evenly.

4. When you're finished, unplug the grinder. Holding the lid in place, turn the grinder upside down and shake the spice mixture into the lid. Pour the garam masala into a small jar with a tight-fitting lid. Store in a cool, dry place for up to 4 weeks.

Goda Masala

VEGAN

PREP TIME: 10 minutes

COOK TIME: 5 minutes

Akin to "Grandma's spices," goda masala seems to show up in as many recipes as there are grandmothers. Interchangeably named *goda*, *kala masala*, or *Maharashtrian*, it is a staple on the dinner table, added to lentils, sprout salads, or rice, and in pinches or by the spoonful in a majority of Maharashtrian homes. My mother taught me about Punjabi garam masala, while my father's mother passed down her knowledge of Maharashtrian goda masala. Yep, it was Grandmother's secret spice recipe! Adjust the black peppercorns and red chiles used in the recipe to your preferred spice level. **MAKES ¼ CUP**

1 tablespoon plus 3 teaspoons peanut oil, divided

½ cup coriander seeds

¼ cup cumin seeds

2 to 3 teaspoons black peppercorns

1 teaspoon whole cloves

3 or 4 cinnamon sticks

¼ cup unsweetened coconut flakes or coconut flour

1 tablespoon sesame seeds

2 or 3 dried red chiles

1. Place a small skillet over medium heat and add 1 tablespoon of oil. Add the coriander seeds, cumin seeds, peppercorns, cloves, and cinnamon. Toast the spices, stirring constantly, until they're fragrant but not browned, about 30 seconds. They burn quickly, so if you're in doubt, undercook them.

2. Transfer the spices to a plate or a paper towel to cool.

3. Meanwhile, add 1 teaspoon of oil to the skillet and toast the coconut flakes for about 30 seconds, until it has a light golden color. Remove the coconut from the pan and add it to the cooling spice mix.

4. Add 1 teaspoon of oil to the pan and toast the sesame seeds, stirring constantly until golden brown, about 30 seconds. Add to the spice mix to cool.

5. Add the remaining 1 teaspoon of oil to the pan and add the chiles. (Make sure the fan is on or that you're in a well-ventilated area.) Toast the chiles very lightly, about 30 seconds. Add to the spice mix to cool.

6. Once all the spices are cool, add them to a spice or coffee grinder. Grind until the spices form a medium-fine powder. Stop the grinder several times and shake it so all the spices get under the blades and grind evenly.

7. When you're finished, unplug the grinder. Holding the lid in place, turn the spice grinder upside down and shake the spice mixture into the lid. Pour the garam masala into a small jar with a tight-fitting lid. Store in a cool, dry location for up to 2 months.

Tip: You can use this for the Masalé Bhat (page 44), as well as for any of the vegetable recipes, as a change from garam masala.

Onion Masala

VEGAN

PREP TIME: 10 minutes

SAUTÉ: 10 minutes

MANUAL: 15 minutes
high pressure

RELEASE: Natural

TOTAL TIME: 60 MINUTES

Onions, tomatoes, ginger, garlic, and a chile, combined with spices, form a masala that is the basis for so many different curries it will set you up for near-instant Indian food for dinner. Traditionally, making it is a labor of love, requiring standing around and stirring frequently. It comes together quickly under pressure, no stirring needed. If I had known you could make this tedious masala this easily, I could have saved me, my mom, my grandmother, and her mother a ton of time in our lives. **MAKES ABOUT 3 CUPS**

¼ cup peanut oil

4 tablespoons
minced garlic

2 tablespoons
minced ginger

1 green serrano or jalapeño
chile, minced

2 cups diced onions

1 teaspoon ground turmeric

½ teaspoon ground
cayenne pepper

2 teaspoons ground cumin

1 teaspoon
ground coriander

2 teaspoons Garam Masala
(page 24)

2 teaspoons salt

1 cup chopped tomato

¼ cup water

1. Preheat the Instant Pot® by selecting Sauté and adjust to More for high heat. When the inner cooking pot is heated, add the oil. When the oil is shimmering, add the garlic, ginger, and green chile, and sauté for 1 to 2 minutes or until fragrant.

2. Add the onions and stir to mix well. Sauté for 6 to 8 minutes, stirring once or twice, until the onions are browned and slightly crisp.

3. Add the turmeric, cayenne, cumin, coriander, garam masala, and salt.

4. Add the chopped tomatoes and water and deglaze the pot well, scraping up all the brown bits. Lock the lid into place.

5. Select Manual and adjust the pressure to High. Cook for 15 minutes. Let the pressure release naturally.

6. Unlock and open the lid. Stir the mixture. The mixture will thicken as it cools. When cool, transfer it to an airtight container. Store in the refrigerator for up to 1 week, or freeze for up to 3 months.

Ghee

VEGETARIAN

PREP TIME: 2 minutes

COOK TIME: 10 minutes

This recipe for ghee rewards you for being lazy. I wish I could say there was a complicated recipe for this, but it's really very simple. Besides, there's nothing better than butter in all its various forms for satiety as well as flavor. I use it to cook veggies, meats, rice . . . everything, really (except maybe bacon). **MAKES 1½ CUPS**

1 pound butter

1. In a heavy-bottomed pan, heat the butter over low heat. Let the butter melt and foam. Don't mess with this too much. It's really not necessary to stir or fuss with it.

2. As the butter stops foaming, the milk solids will start to turn brown and settle into the bottom of the pan. The browning is necessary to create the authentic, slightly nutty taste of ghee.

3. When the butter is well browned, remove the pan from the heat, let the ghee cool a little, and pour it through a fine strainer into a jar and close with a lid. Ghee doesn't require refrigeration and is shelf-stable, so leave it on your counter for easy access for cooking.

Ginger-Garlic Paste

VEGAN

PREP TIME: 5 minutes

Tip: In recipes that call for 2 teaspoons of garlic and 1 teaspoon of ginger, just use 1 tablespoon of this paste, fresh or frozen.

Having your own ginger–garlic paste on hand will make a lot of these recipes go faster. Commercial blends contain fillers and oil, and over time the oil changes the flavor of the paste. **MAKES ¾ CUP**

¼ cup water

½ cup peeled garlic cloves

½ cup sliced ginger (no need to peel)

1. Into a blender jar or food processor, pour the water to help the blades move freely.

2. Add the garlic and ginger, and process until the mixture is relatively smooth.

3. Store in the refrigerator in an airtight container for 2 to 3 weeks, or freeze the mixture by scooping 1 tablespoon into each cube of an ice cube tray. Once they are frozen, pop the tablespoons out into a zip-top bag and keep in the freezer.

Paneer

PREP TIME: 10 minutes

MANUAL: 4 minutes
low pressure

RELEASE: Natural
10 minutes, then Quick

**TOTAL TIME: 35 MINUTES, PLUS
1 TO 2 HOURS TO DRAIN**

In the search for vegetarian protein in India, paneer came to existence. Beginning with water-buffalo milk or cow milk, the traditional recipe is time-consuming and demanding of your attention. The Instant Pot® eases those requirements and also produces more paneer from the milk. Sounds like a classic win-win!

MAKES ABOUT 1½ CUPS

1 quart half-and-half   ¼ cup white vinegar

1. In the inner cooking pot of the Instant Pot®, combine the half-and-half and vinegar. Lock the lid into place.

2. Select Manual and adjust the pressure to Low. Cook at low pressure for 4 minutes. Allow the pressure to release naturally for 10 minutes, then quick-release any remaining pressure.

3. Unlock the lid. When you open the pot, the milk will have separated into curds and a watery whey. Stir the contents of the pot well.

4. Line a sieve or mold with cheesecloth and place it over a bowl (the bowl will collect the whey, which you can save for other uses). Pour the paneer into the sieve, gather up the cheesecloth over the top of the paneer, and put a heavy weight on it to let the whey drain thoroughly for 1 to 2 hours. The paneer will form a cohesive block or ball.

5. Wrap the paneer in plastic wrap. Refrigerate it in an airtight container for up to 2 days.

Greek Yogurt

PREP TIME: 5 minutes

YOGURT: 8 hours

TOTAL TIME: 8 HOURS,
5 MINUTES, PLUS OVERNIGHT
TO DRAIN

Once you make Greek yogurt at home, you will understand why the Instant Pot® has so many yogurt-making aficionados. The yogurt is thick, creamy, and needs little to make it utterly delicious.
MAKES ABOUT 2 CUPS

2 cups whole milk

2 tablespoons store-bought Greek yogurt starter

1. In a small microwave-safe bowl, heat the milk in the microwave for 2 minutes. Carefully test its temperature with your finger. The milk should feel warm but not enough to burn you (about 110°F).

2. In another small bowl, add the yogurt starter and ½ cup of the warm milk. Mix until the starter is well dissolved, then pour into the warm milk and mix again.

3. Transfer the mixture into a mason jar, a ceramic crock, or some other container that is heatproof and will fit into your Instant Pot®. I use pint-size mason jars, but you can also make the yogurt directly in the inner pot.

4. Place the jar in the inner cooking pot of the Instant Pot®. Press the Yogurt button, set the timer for 8 hours, and place a glass lid on the pot. If you're using the lid that came with the pot, position the release valve to Venting, not Sealing, to make the yogurt.

5. Once the yogurt is set, place a cheesecloth or a large coffee filter over a large stainless steel strainer, place the strainer over a bowl, and let it drip in the refrigerator overnight. Transfer the yogurt to an airtight container and store refrigerated for up to 2 weeks.

Greek Yogurt in Popular Indian Foods

Most Indian homes have one last ritual before bedtime—setting yogurt out to incubate. Yogurt is served with meals and often eaten at the end of a meal. It cools spicy foods, tenderizes meat, mixes well with salads or rice, and often signifies the end of a meal. We also use yogurt to create cooling drinks such as lassi. Pro tip: Do not pronounce *lassi* like you would the famous TV dog Lassie. It's pronounced *lussi*.

CUCUMBER RAITA

SERVES 4 / PREP TIME: 15 MINUTES

1 medium cucumber, peeled and grated
1 cup Greek Yogurt (previous page)
Salt
Freshly ground black pepper
2 teaspoons chopped fresh cilantro (optional)
½ teaspoon chopped fresh mint (optional)
¼ teaspoon ground cumin (optional)

In a small bowl, combine all of the ingredients and chill them until ready to serve.

Tip: Vary this basic recipe by adding diced tomatoes and diced onions along with the cucumbers.

BASIC LASSI WITH VARIATIONS

SERVES 2 / PREP TIME: 5 MINUTES

1½ cups Greek Yogurt (previous page)
1 cup water
½ cup ice cubes
1 teaspoon salt, plus more for seasoning

In a blender jar, add all of the ingredients and process until smooth. Taste and adjust the seasoning, adding more salt as needed.

Variations

Sweet Lassi: Replace the salt with 2 teaspoons (or more) of sugar or sweetener.

Mango Lassi: Omit the salt and add 1 cup of ripe mango cubes and ¼ teaspoon of cardamom.

Savory Lassi: Dry-roast cumin seeds, grind them, and add ½ teaspoon of the ground cumin during blending.

Spicy Lassi: Add 2 or 3 thin ginger slices, 2 slices of serrano chile, and ⅛ cup of chopped fresh cilantro.

Banana Lassi: Omit the salt and add 1 banana, along with some additional sugar if needed.

What the Heck Is This Yumminess Lassi: Add ½ teaspoon of ready-made chaat masala.

Mint Lassi: Add ½ teaspoon of dried mint.

Papaya Lassi: Omit the salt and add 1 cup of papaya chunks and ¼ teaspoon of cardamom.

Meyer Lemon Chutney

VEGAN

PREP TIME: 10 minutes

MANUAL: 15 minutes
high pressure

SAUTÉ: 5 minutes

RELEASE: Natural
10 minutes, then Quick

TOTAL TIME: 60 MINUTES

Freshly made chutneys are a wonderful way to enhance flavors at the table. Ideally, a chutney is a blend of flavors that includes salty, spicy hot, tangy, and sweet. Meyer lemons allow the use of the entire fruit, including the soft edible skin. This raita is an excellent addition to the flavor of grilled meat, or as a condiment in sandwiches. It makes my mouth water just thinking about it. **MAKES 1½ CUPS**

2½ cups chopped Meyer lemons, rinds and flesh

½ small onion, diced

¾ cup raw sugar or brown sugar

¼ cup vinegar

¼ cup raisins

1 tablespoon diced ginger

1 teaspoon salt

¼ teaspoon ground cayenne pepper

⅛ teaspoon ground cumin

1. In the inner cooking pot of the Instant Pot®, combine all of the ingredients. Lock the lid into place.

2. Select Manual and adjust the pressure to High. Cook for 15 minutes. Allow the pot to release pressure naturally for 10 minutes, then quick-release any remaining pressure.

3. Unlock and remove the lid. Stir and taste the chutney, adjusting any spices as necessary.

4. Select Sauté and adjust to More for high heat. Let the chutney boil for another 3 to 5 minutes to get rid of any excess water. It will continue to thicken as it cools.

5. Transfer the chutney to an airtight storage container and refrigerate for up to 3 weeks.

Coconut Green Chutney

VEGAN

PREP TIME: 25 minutes

I really like recipes that make up part of one meal and then can be used to create something entirely different for the next meal. This chutney is one of those types of recipes. Chutneys are used as condiments, and this is a favorite that combines rich coconut flavor with cilantro, mint, garlic, and serrano pepper. It is one of the most popular sides in Indian cooking. I grew up eating it on tomato and cucumber sandwiches. **MAKES 1 CUP**

½ cup unsweetened shredded coconut

½ cup hot water

6 garlic cloves, chopped

½ to 1 serrano or jalapeño chile, chopped

2 cups chopped fresh cilantro

¼ cup chopped fresh mint

Juice of 1 lemon

¼ to ¾ cup water, as needed

1. In the jar of a blender or bowl of a food processor, place the coconut and add the hot water. Let the coconut soak for about 5 minutes while you prepare the other ingredients.

2. Add the garlic and chile to the blender. Add the cilantro, mint, lemon juice, and an additional ¼ cup of water. Blend at low speed, stopping the blender occasionally to tamp down the ingredients. Add water sparingly to keep the contents moving, as needed.

3. Once the contents are moving freely, turn the blender to high and process until the chutney is puréed.

Mango Chutney

VEGAN

PREP TIME: 10 minutes

COOK TIME: 1 minute

TOTAL TIME: 11 MINUTES,
PLUS 15 MINUTES TO
LET FLAVORS BLEND

As a child, I was sent with my cousins into the back-yard in our underwear to eat ripe mangos from the trees. Then we'd hose ourselves off to remove all the sticky juice before we were allowed back into the house. Children and ripe mangos are a messy combination. However, unripe mangos, with their tartness, are used in a variety of ways. One is this simple recipe for mango chutney. These few ingredients, which can be combined at the last minute, will add a tangy zip to an otherwise ordinary meal. Serve with any Indian main dish, or with fish or grilled meat. This chutney also makes a great dip for sweet-potato fries. **MAKES 1 CUP**

½ cup peeled and grated unripe green mango

½ cup chopped onion

2 teaspoons sugar or honey, or more to taste

½ teaspoon ground cayenne pepper, or more to taste

½ teaspoon ground roasted cumin

½ teaspoon salt

2 teaspoons peanut oil

¼ teaspoon black mustard seeds or cumin seeds

1. In a small bowl, combine the mango and onion, and mix well.

2. Add the sugar, cayenne, cumin, and salt, and taste. You want a good balance of hot, salty, tart, and sweet. Since mangos vary in their tartness, adjust the sugar as needed.

3. In a small saucepan over high heat, heat the oil. When it starts to shimmer, add the mustard seeds and let them pop. This allows the mustard seeds to bloom in flavor while also infusing the oil.

4. Once the seeds have sputtered for about 10 seconds, pour the flavored oil onto the chutney and mix well.

5. Let the flavors blend for 10 to 15 minutes before serving.

Tip: Black mustard seeds are the most pungent of all mustard seeds. The tiny seeds are dark brown, sometimes with a slightly reddish hue. They can be found in Indian or international markets, or online.

LANGAR KI DAL, PAGE 52

CHAPTER 3

Rice, Dals & Beans

Basmati Pilau

PREP TIME: 15 minutes

SAUTÉ: 10 minutes

MANUAL: 5 minutes
high pressure

RELEASE: Natural
10 minutes, then Quick

TOTAL TIME: 50 MINUTES

This fragrant rice, studded with spices and redolent with ghee and fried onions, is a perfect accompaniment to your Indian meal. Traditionally, whole spices are found scattered through the finished dish, and in India we are trained from a young age to eat around whole spices. Rather than risking a bite directly into a peppercorn, this recipe asks you to use a muslin bag to hold all the spices, ensuring you get all the taste without the possible inconvenience. **SERVES 4**

3 or 4 green
cardamom pods

6 to 8 black peppercorns

4 whole cloves

2-inch piece cinnamon stick

1 tablespoon Ghee
(page 30)

½ teaspoon cumin seeds

1 cup thinly sliced red onion

1 teaspoon salt

1 cup basmati rice, rinsed
and drained

1¼ cups water

1. Put the cardamom pods, peppercorns, cloves, and cinnamon into a muslin bag or a spice infuser and crush slightly.

2. Preheat the Instant Pot® by selecting Sauté and adjust to More for high heat. When the inner cooking pot is hot, add the ghee and heat until it is shimmering. Add the cumin seeds and cook for about 30 seconds, or until they begin to sputter. It will sound like popcorn beginning to pop.

3. Add the sliced onion and salt, and cook, stirring, until the edges of the onion pieces are browned and crisp. You want them well cooked but not burned.

4. Add the rice and mix until each grain is coated with ghee. Add the spice bag and water.

5. Lock the lid into place. Select Manual and adjust the pressure to High. Cook for 5 minutes. When cooking is complete, let the pressure release naturally for 10 minutes, then quick-release any remaining pressure.

6. Unlock the lid and serve.

Tip: If you like, add ⅓ cup of green peas after the pressure is released, but before the final steaming.

Masalé Bhat MARATHI SPICED RICE

VEGETARIAN

PREP TIME: 10 minutes

SAUTÉ: 3 minutes

RICE/MANUAL: 12 minutes
low pressure

RELEASE: Natural
10 minutes, then Quick

TOTAL TIME: 45 MINUTES

When I visit India, my family wants to know what they can make for me. Masalé bhat is always at the top of my list. This is without a doubt one of my favorite ways to eat rice. I may waver between this recipe and the Chicken Biryani (page 96), but they are really two different things. This dish contains the Goda Masala (page 26). It is worth the small effort it takes. It is rarely served outside of India, so by making it, you will be bringing into your home a little slice of Indian culture that you might not otherwise experience. **SERVES 6**

1 tablespoon Ghee
(page 30) or peanut oil

¼ teaspoon cumin seeds

¼ teaspoon black mustard
seeds (omit if you don't
have them)

1 cup chopped mixed
vegetables (see Tip)

1 cup basmati rice, rinsed
and drained

1¼ cups water

1 teaspoon salt

2 tablespoons Goda Masala
(page 26)

¼ teaspoon
ground turmeric

¼ cup Spanish peanuts or
other roasted peanuts

¼ cup chopped
fresh cilantro

1. Preheat the Instant Pot® by selecting Sauté and adjusting to More for high heat. When the inner cooking pot is hot, add the ghee and heat until it is shimmering. Add the cumin seeds and mustard seeds and cook for about 1 minute, or until they start sputtering like popcorn popping.

2. Add the vegetables and stir to coat with the flavored ghee.

3. Add the rice, water, salt, goda masala, turmeric, and peanuts.

4. Lock the lid into place. Select the Rice setting (or select Manual, adjust the pressure to Low, and set the time for 12 minutes).

5. When the cooking is complete, let the pressure release naturally for 10 minutes, then quick-release any remaining pressure.

6. Stir in the chopped cilantro and serve. This dish goes well with the Coconut-Tomato Soup (page 78).

Tip: Some veggies you can use include cauliflower, peas, green beans, cabbage, broccoli, and mushrooms.

Khichadi RICE WITH LENTILS

VEGETARIAN

PREP TIME: 10 minutes

SAUTÉ: 1 minute

MANUAL: 10 minutes
high pressure

RELEASE: Natural

TOTAL TIME: 45 MINUTES

In my youth, whenever I felt ill, I would ask my mother for simple khichadi. The Indian equivalent of grilled cheese and tomato soup, khichadi is the comfort food for rough days or when you're feeling under the weather. It's rice and dal, cooked together in a pressure cooker until it forms a mush. Flavored with ghee, cumin seeds, turmeric, and salt, khichadi is eaten by very small babies, who grow up eating this easily digested meal. I love to add peanuts, as I've done in this version. **SERVES 6**

¾ cup short-grain rice

¼ cup moong dal or any split dal, or a mix

1 tablespoon Ghee (page 30), plus more for serving

1 teaspoon cumin seeds

½ teaspoon ground turmeric

¼ cup Spanish red or other roasted peanuts

1¾ cups water, plus more as needed

1 teaspoon salt

Yogurt, for serving (optional)

1. Mix the rice and dal and place in a sieve. Rinse well under running water.

2. Preheat the Instant Pot® by selecting Sauté and adjust to More for high heat. When the inner pot is hot, add the ghee and heat until it is shimmering. Add the cumin seeds and cook for about 1 minute, or until they start sputtering like popcorn popping.

3. Add the turmeric and let it sizzle for a few seconds. Quickly add the peanuts and stir. Add the rice and dal, and stir until all of it is coated with the ghee. Pour in the water and add the salt.

4. Lock the lid into place. Select Manual and adjust the pressure to High. Cook for 10 minutes.

5. When the cooking is complete, let the pressure release naturally. Unlock the lid.

6. If the rice has absorbed all the liquid, add up to ¼ cup of water, or until the consistency resembles oatmeal.

7. Stir everything together and serve with additional ghee or a little yogurt on the side.

Dal Fry LENTILS WITH FRIED ONIONS

VEGETARIAN

PREP TIME: 15 minutes

MANUAL: 6 minutes
high pressure

COOK TIME: 20 minutes

RELEASE: Natural

TOTAL TIME: 1 HOUR 5 MINUTES

Dal fry is a popular recipe, and with good reason. A creamy combination of dal, crisp caramelized onions flavored with ghee and cumin, and tomato, the dish produces a complex range of flavors for such a simple recipe. You can make this with any kind of split dal, such as tuvar, masoor, or moong. **SERVES 4**

2¾ cups water, divided

½ cup chana dal (or any split dal)

2 teaspoons Ghee (page 30)

¼ teaspoon cumin seeds

2 dried red chiles

4 garlic cloves, minced

1 cup thinly sliced red onion

1 large tomato, chopped

½ teaspoon ground turmeric

1 teaspoon salt

½ teaspoon ground cumin

¼ cup chopped fresh cilantro

1. Pour 1 cup of water into the inner cooking pot of the Instant Pot®, then place a trivet in the pot.

2. In a heatproof bowl that fits inside the Instant Pot®, combine the dal and 1 cup of water. Place the bowl on the trivet.

3. Lock the lid into place. Select Manual and adjust the pressure to High. Cook for 6 minutes. When the cooking is complete, let the pressure release naturally. Unlock the lid.

4. While the chana dal cooks, heat a medium saucepan over medium-high heat on the stove top. Add the ghee. When it shimmers, add the cumin seeds, red chiles, and garlic and cook for 1 minute.

5. Add the onion slices and cook, stirring occasionally, until the onions are crisp and lightly browned, 5 to 8 minutes.

6. Add the tomato and let it heat through as you gently mash it with the back of your spoon. Sprinkle in the turmeric, salt, and cumin, mixing well.

7. When the dal is finished, carefully remove the bowl from the pressure cooker. Transfer the dal to the saucepan and add the remaining ¾ cup of water. Stir to combine. Turn the heat to low and let it simmer for 5 to 10 minutes, or until the flavors meld. Garnish with the cilantro and serve.

Dal Makhani CREAMY LENTILS

VEGETARIAN

PREP TIME: 15 minutes

MANUAL: 30 minutes
high pressure

COOK TIME: 2 minutes

RELEASE: Natural

TOTAL TIME: 1 HOUR 10 MINUTES

Dal makhani or maa ki daal (Mother's dal, the epitome of comfort food) traditionally requires hours upon hours of slow cooking to bring the lentils to the perfectly soft and creamy stage. Enter Instant Pot®, and 30 minutes later you can imagine your mother serving you a bowl of this incredibly pleasing dish. Unlike using onion masala or some other thickener to the dal, the lentils themselves break down in absolute creamy goodness. **SERVES 4**

FOR THE DAL

½ cup whole black urad dal

2 bay leaves

1 tablespoon chopped garlic

2 teaspoons minced ginger

2½ cups water

¼ cup Greek yogurt

½ cup half-and-half or cream (or a nondairy milk of your choice)

1 teaspoon salt

½ teaspoon ground turmeric

¼ teaspoon ground cayenne pepper

¼ teaspoon ground cumin

½ teaspoon ground coriander

½ teaspoon Garam Masala (page 24)

FOR FINISHING THE DAL

2 teaspoons Ghee (page 30)

1 teaspoon cumin seeds

1 tablespoon tomato paste

Chopped fresh cilantro, for garnish (optional)

TO MAKE THE DAL

1. Rinse the dal well and transfer it to the inner cooking pot of the Instant Pot®. Add the bay leaves, garlic, ginger, and water.

2. Lock the lid into place. Select Manual and adjust the pressure to High. Cook for 30 minutes. When the cooking is complete, let the pressure release naturally.

3. Meanwhile, in a small bowl, stir together the yogurt, half-and-half, salt, turmeric, cayenne, cumin, coriander, and garam masala. Mix thoroughly and set aside.

4. When the dal is ready, unlock and remove the lid. Using the back of a spoon, gently mash some of the dal to make a thicker mixture, leaving most of it intact.

5. Select the Warm setting.

TO FINISH THE DAL

1. In a small saucepan, heat the ghee over medium heat until it shimmers, and add the cumin seeds, which will start to sputter. Add the tomato paste and cook, stirring, until it absorbs all the ghee, about 2 minutes. Pour this paste into the dal and mix well.

2. Add the yogurt mixture and mix well. Serve garnished with the chopped cilantro (if using).

Tip: Serve with naan, chapatis, or rice, or eat the dal plain by the spoonful, which is what I do.

Langar Ki Dal CREAMY MIXED LENTILS

VEGETARIAN

PREP TIME: 10 minutes

BEAN/CHILI: 30 minutes high pressure

COOK TIME: 8 minutes

RELEASE: Natural 10 minutes, then Quick

TOTAL TIME: 1 HOUR, 10 MINUTES

Langar is a Punjabi word for the community kitchen or meal, made and served by volunteers at the *gurdwara* ("temple"). All are welcome to this delicious, free meal. This food was much of the reason my brother and I looked forward to going to the gurdwara. As part of a religious ceremony, visiting the gurdwara should not be about taste, but they make the food so appetizing. This dal is a classic offering from the langar, and I feel fortunate to be able to make it and share it at home. **SERVES 8**

FOR THE DAL

1 cup whole black urad dal

½ cup chana dal

5 cups water

1 teaspoon salt

1 teaspoon ground turmeric

FOR FINISHING THE DAL

1 tablespoon Ghee (page 30) (or substitute coconut oil or vegetable oil)

1 onion, chopped

1 tablespoon minced ginger

1 tablespoon minced garlic

2 tomatoes, chopped

½ teaspoon cumin seeds

½ teaspoon ground turmeric

½ teaspoon ground cayenne pepper, or more to taste

1 teaspoon salt

¼ cup water

1. In the inner cooking pot of the Instant Pot®, combine the urad and chana dals. Add the water, salt, and turmeric, and stir to combine.

2. Lock the lid into place. Select the Bean/Chili setting and adjust the pressure to High and the time to 30 minutes.

3. Allow the pressure to release naturally for 10 minutes, then quick-release any remaining pressure. Unlock and remove the lid.

4. Using a spoon, crush the dals well to get a creamier texture, leaving some whole dal in the mixture.

TO FINISH THE DAL

1. While the dals are cooking, heat a nonstick pan on the stove top over medium-high heat. When the pan is hot, add the ghee. When the ghee is shimmering, add the onion and sauté for 30 seconds. Add the ginger and garlic and cook for 5 minutes until the edges of the onion start to brown slightly.

2. Add the tomatoes, cumin seeds, turmeric, cayenne, and salt, and mix well. Add the water and mix again. Cook, crushing the tomatoes with the back of a spoon, for 1 to 2 minutes. Set aside until the dals are cooked.

3. When the dals have finished cooking, pour in the tomato-and-onion mixture and mix well before serving.

Chana Masala

PREP TIME: 10 minutes, plus 1 hour to soak

MANUAL: 18 minutes high pressure

SAUTÉ: 3 minutes

RELEASE: Natural

TOTAL TIME: 55 MINUTES, PLUS TIME TO SOAK

A favorite among home cooks in India, chana masala is also sold everywhere from expensive restaurants to hawkers at railroad stations. Restaurants often use brewed tea to impart a darker flavor to the final dish. You can do that, but most home cooks skip that step, which adds color but not much flavor. This recipe tastes exactly like the chana masala my mom made. I'm happy to offer you something close to what she would have made for you if you came by our house at lunchtime. **SERVES 6**

1 cup dried chickpeas

2 to 3 bay leaves

3 cups water

1 tablespoon Ghee (page 30)

⅓ cup Onion Masala (page 28)

2 teaspoons ready-made chana masala powder

1 teaspoon salt

Juice of 1 lemon

¼ cup chopped fresh cilantro

Continued

1. In the inner cooking pot of the Instant Pot®, combine the chickpeas, bay leaves, and water.

2. Lock the lid into place. Select Manual and adjust the pressure to High. Cook for 18 minutes. When the cooking is complete, let the pressure release naturally. Unlock the lid.

3. Carefully remove the lid and drain the chickpeas, reserving the cooking water. Transfer the chickpeas to a medium bowl.

4. Using a potato masher, roughly mash about half of the chickpeas. This will thicken the final sauce. Set aside.

Ready-Made Chana Masala Powder

I encourage you to cook everything from scratch and to make your own spice blends. Even so, I call for chana masala as a ready-made spice blend. The list of ingredients required to make a good chana masala is lengthy and formidable. From hard-to-find ingredients like pomegranate seeds, dried mango powder, and dried fenugreek leaves to ingredients you need only a pinch of, such as dried ginger, asafetida, and fennel, it would take you longer to find the ingredients for this mix than to make the chana! Indian home cooks buy ready-made chana masala powder, and if you want authentic taste at home, I suggest you do the same. Ask at your local Indian grocery store, or look online for brands that are well rated, such as MTR and Shan, and save your time to make a lovely dessert to follow your meal instead.

5. Rinse and dry the inner cooking pot. Replace it in the Instant Pot®.

6. Preheat the Instant Pot® by selecting Sauté and adjust to More for high heat. When the pot is hot, add the ghee. When it is shimmering, add the onion masala. Sauté for 2 to 3 minutes until the masala is heated through, then add the chana masala powder and salt. Mix well.

7. Add the chickpeas and enough of the cooking water to achieve the consistency of oatmeal, and heat through.

8. Stir in the lemon juice.

9. Garnish with the cilantro and serve with rice, naan, or chapatis.

Tip: In an authentic chana masala, ½ teaspoon of amchoor powder would be used in place of the lemon juice. Amchoor is ground dried mango, which is slightly sour. It can be found in Indian or international markets.

Chana Salaad CHICKPEA SALAD

VEGAN

PREP TIME: 10 minutes

BEAN/CHILI: 20 minutes
high pressure

RELEASE: Natural
10 minutes, then Quick

TOTAL TIME: 50 MINUTES

I think my mom lied to me about this chana salaad. She said it was junk food so I would eat it, but now that I'm older I know better. After all, it's chickpeas and vegetables! But I'm glad my mom said whatever it took at the time to get me to eat it, because I love this salad. It is perfect for summer and is easy to make. Serve it as a side salad or as a main dish for a vegan meal. Adjust the cayenne as desired for your heat preference. **SERVES 6**

1 cup dried chickpeas

3 bay leaves

3 cups water

1 cup finely minced
red onion

½ cup diced tomato

½ cup chopped
fresh cilantro

1 teaspoon salt

½ teaspoon ground
cayenne pepper

¼ cup freshly squeezed
lemon juice

1. In the inner cooking pot of the Instant Pot®, combine the chickpeas, bay leaves, and water.

2. Lock the lid into place. Select the Bean/Chili setting and adjust the pressure to High and the time to 20 minutes.

3. After cooking, allow the pressure to release naturally for 10 minutes, then quick-release any remaining pressure. Unlock and remove the lid.

4. While the chickpeas are cooling, in a large bowl, combine the onion, tomato, and cilantro.

5. Drain the chickpeas and add them to the vegetables. Add the salt, cayenne, and lemon juice. Mix well and taste, adjusting the seasoning as needed. You want a good mix of tangy, salty, and spicy.

Tip: To vary the flavor, add any of the following: ½ teaspoon of chaat masala, ½ teaspoon of amchoor (dried mango powder), or ¼ teaspoon of kala namaak (volcanic black salt with a slightly sulfuric smell).

Punjabi Lobia BLACK-EYED PEAS WITH SPINACH

VEGETARIAN

PREP TIME: 10 minutes

SAUTÉ: 3 minutes

MANUAL: 10 minutes
high pressure

RELEASE: Natural
10 minutes, then Quick

TOTAL TIME: 45 MINUTES

Whenever I was feeling particularly lazy, I would make Punjabi lobia. I would use canned beans, and the taste would be okay. Then I realized that you could make perfectly cooked black-eyed peas in 10 minutes in a pressure cooker. Now we have this meal much more often, and it is so much better. Chop one tomato, and everything else is pour and cook. The end result is a creamy, full-bodied bean and spinach dish that makes an excellent weeknight supper. As always, adjust the cayenne to your heat preference. **SERVES 6**

1 tablespoon Ghee
(page 30) or peanut oil

⅛ teaspoon cumin seeds

⅛ teaspoon black mustard seeds (or omit and double up on the cumin seeds)

1 tablespoon minced garlic

1 tablespoon minced ginger

1 cup diced tomato

½ teaspoon
ground turmeric

¼ teaspoon ground
cayenne pepper

½ teaspoon ground cumin

½ teaspoon
ground coriander

1 teaspoon salt

1 cup dried black-eyed peas

2 cups water

4 cups raw spinach

1. Preheat the Instant Pot® by selecting Sauté and adjusting to More for high heat. When the inner cooking pot is hot, add the ghee and heat until it is shimmering, then add the cumin seeds and mustard seeds (if using). They will begin to sputter like popcorn popping. Add the garlic and ginger and sauté for 30 seconds.

2. Add the tomato and cook for 1 to 2 minutes until the tomato has softened.

3. Add the turmeric, cayenne, cumin, coriander, and salt, and mix well.

4. Add the black-eyed peas and water, and mix. Place the spinach on top.

5. Lock the lid into place. Select Manual and adjust the pressure to High. Cook for 10 minutes. Allow 10 minutes of natural pressure release, then quick-release any remaining pressure.

6. When the cooking is complete, unlock and remove the lid. Stir and taste, adding more salt or cayenne if necessary. Serve with rice, chapatis, or naan.

Matki Chi Ussal SPICED SPROUTED BEANS

VEGAN

PREP TIME: 10 minutes

SAUTÉ: 2 minutes

MANUAL: 4 minutes
high pressure

RELEASE: Quick

TOTAL TIME: 25 MINUTES

I was a fussy eater as a child. I'd eat junk food, especially if it was savory, but convincing me to eat vegetables was a daily tussle. This matki ussal, however, was an altogether different matter. The beans are small and cute, have little tails, are delicious, and are easily digested when sprouted. This is a traditional Maharashtrian dish. Irresistible little beans, coconut, cilantro, and a little sugar. What's not to love? Scale up or down the cayenne pepper for your heat preference. **SERVES 6**

1 tablespoon peanut oil

1 teaspoon cumin seeds or black mustard seeds

½ cup chopped onion

½ cup chopped tomato

3 garlic cloves, minced

1 teaspoon minced ginger

1 cup sprouted beans (about ½ cup dried moth beans, sprouted; see Tip)

¼ cup unsweetened shredded coconut

1 teaspoon salt

½ teaspoon ground turmeric

¼ teaspoon ground cayenne pepper

1 teaspoon ground coriander

½ teaspoon ground cumin

½ cup water

¼ cup chopped fresh cilantro

¼ cup fresh grated coconut (optional)

1. Preheat the Instant Pot® by selecting Sauté and adjusting to More for high heat. When the pot is hot, add the oil and heat until it is shimmering. Add the cumin seeds and let them sputter like popcorn popping.

2. Add the onion, tomato, garlic, and ginger, and sauté for 2 minutes until the onion is soft and translucent.

3. Add the sprouted beans, coconut, salt, turmeric, cayenne, coriander, cumin, and water, and stir to combine.

4. Lock the lid into place. Select Manual and adjust the pressure to High. Cook for 4 minutes.

5. When the cooking is complete, quick-release the pressure.

6. Unlock and remove the lid. Garnish with cilantro and fresh coconut (if using).

Tip: Sprouting beans is easy but requires preplanning. To sprout beans in your Instant Pot®, first soak 1 cup of dried moth beans for 3 to 4 hours in 2 cups of very hot or boiling water. Into a steaming basket over the Instant Pot® pour the beans and any remaining water, allowing the water to drip to the bottom of the pot. Set the Instant Pot® to Yogurt and the timer for 8 hours. The beans should be well sprouted after that and will have small tails emerging from them. If not, start the Yogurt cycle again and check halfway through for doneness.

Punjabi Rajma RED KIDNEY BEANS

VEGAN

PREP TIME: 10 minutes

BEAN/CHILI: 30 minutes
high pressure

SAUTÉ: 5 minutes

RELEASE: Natural
10 minutes, then Quick

TOTAL TIME: 1 HOUR 5 MINUTES

Every Punjabi household has its own version of rajma, and nothing says comfort food like this dish. It's what you cook on a day you're tired and can't be bothered to cook too much. This dish is made considerably easier if you already have the Onion Masala (page 28) on hand (see Tip), but you can always make them together, which is what the recipe calls for. It's also a recipe you can adapt with your favorite type of beans. **SERVES 6**

1 tablespoon peanut oil

1½ cups diced onion

1 tablespoon minced ginger

1 tablespoon minced garlic

1 cup diced tomato

1 teaspoon ground
cayenne pepper

1 teaspoon ground turmeric

1 teaspoon Garam Masala
(page 24)

1 teaspoon ground cumin

1 teaspoon salt

1 teaspoon
ground coriander

1 cup dried red kidney beans

2 cups water

1. Put the oil into the inner cooking pot of the Instant Pot®, and add the onion, ginger, garlic, tomato, cayenne, turmeric, garam masala, cumin, salt, and coriander. Stir to combine.

2. Place a trivet on top of the onion mixture.

3. Put the beans and water into a heatproof bowl. Cover the bowl with foil. Place the covered bowl on top of the trivet.

4. Lock the lid into place. Select the Bean/Chili setting and adjust the pressure to High and the time to 30 minutes.

5. After cooking, let the pressure release naturally for 10 minutes, then quick-release any remaining pressure.

6. Unlock and remove the lid. Carefully remove the bowl of red kidney beans and the trivet.

7. Slightly mash about half the beans with the back of a spoon.

8. Turn the Instant Pot® off, then select Sauté and adjust to More for high heat. Pour the beans and any remaining liquid into the onion masala and mix well. Let the contents come to a boil to meld all the flavors well, about 5 minutes.

Tip: If you have Onion Masala on hand, you can skip steps 1 and 2 and proceed with the rest of the recipe.

ALOO GOBI, PAGE 68

CHAPTER 4

Vegetables & Vegetarian

Aloo Gobi POTATOES AND CAULIFLOWER

VEGAN

PREP TIME: 15 minutes

SAUTÉ: 11 minutes

MANUAL: 2 minutes
low pressure

RELEASE: Quick

TOTAL TIME: 40 MINUTES

Aloo gobi is standard fare in Indian restaurants, and it is a mainstay in Punjabi households. The potatoes and cauliflower blend together perfectly with a host of herbs. The stalks of the cauliflower are called "danthal" and are considered wonderful additions to this dish. Do leave the cauliflower florets on the large side to prevent overcooking. You can always break them up gently once they're cooked. **SERVES 4**

1 tablespoon peanut oil

1 teaspoon cumin seeds

2 cups sliced potatoes, about ¼ inch thick

1 teaspoon salt

1 teaspoon Garam Masala (page 24)

½ teaspoon ground turmeric

¼ teaspoon ground cumin

½ teaspoon ground coriander

¼ teaspoon ground cayenne pepper

½ cup diced tomato

¼ cup water

4 cups large cauliflower florets (about 1 medium cauliflower)

2 teaspoons chopped fresh cilantro, for garnish (optional)

1. Preheat the Instant Pot® by selecting Sauté and adjust to More for high heat. When the inner cooking pot is hot, add the oil and heat until shimmering. Add the cumin seeds and stir. They'll sputter like popcorn popping.

2. Add the potatoes and sauté, stirring occasionally, for 2 to 3 minutes, or until they begin to brown and crisp a little.

3. Add the salt, garam masala, turmeric, cumin, coriander, and cayenne, and sauté for 1 minute. Add the tomato and water, and stir, scraping up all the lovely fond on the bottom of the pot. Add the cauliflower and stir gently.

4. Lock the lid into place. Select Manual and adjust the pressure to Low. Cook for 2 minutes.

5. When the cooking is complete, quick-release the pressure. Unlock the lid.

6. Garnish with the chopped cilantro (if using).

Aloo Jeera CUMIN-SPICED POTATOES

VEGETARIAN

PREP TIME: 10 minutes

STEAM: 6 minutes on high

SAUTÉ: 1 minute

RELEASE: Quick

TOTAL TIME: 30 MINUTES

You will likely look at this recipe and think I have accidentally left out some ingredients. How can something this simple result in anything that tastes good? I urge you to try it exactly as written the first time, and experience the wonderful blend of simple flavors. This humble dish, which derives its rich flavor from the ghee, cumin, and chiles, can be eaten as an accompaniment to any meal. **SERVES 4**

2 cups water

2 cups cubed potatoes

1 tablespoon Ghee (page 30)

½ serrano chile, cut into thick slices

½ teaspoon cumin seeds

¼ teaspoon ground turmeric (optional)

1 teaspoon salt

¼ cup chopped fresh cilantro, for garnish

1. Into the inner cooking pot of the Instant Pot®, pour the water, and place a steamer basket inside. Put the cubed potatoes in the steamer basket.

2. Lock the lid into place, select Steam, and adjust the pressure to High. Cook for 6 minutes. When the cooking is complete, quick-release the pressure.

3. Unlock and remove the lid. Carefully remove the steamer basket and set the potatoes aside. Rinse and dry the inner liner. Place it back into the Instant Pot®.

4. Preheat the Instant Pot® by selecting Sauté and adjusting to More for high heat. When the pot is hot, add the ghee and heat until it is shimmering. Add the serrano pepper and cumin seeds, and let the seeds sputter and cook for about 15 seconds.

5. Add the turmeric (if using) and stir to mix. Add the potatoes and salt, and mix gently to coat the potatoes with the flavored ghee, taking care to not break them.

6. Garnish with the cilantro and serve.

Beet Koshimbir BEETROOT SALAD

VEGETARIAN

PREP TIME: 10 minutes

MANUAL: 12 minutes
high pressure

COOK TIME: 1 minute

RELEASE: Natural

TOTAL TIME: 50 MINUTES,
PLUS 1 HOUR TO CHILL

If you've never cooked beets in the Instant Pot®, you're in for a treat. Not only do they cook perfectly, but after cooking, the peels slide off with almost no effort. Maharashtrian meals often include a koshimbir, a cold vegetable salad. The koshimbir can be made with a variety of vegetables and usually includes roasted and chopped peanuts, cilantro, and yogurt or lime juice. Replace the beets with finely chopped cucumbers or green beans for a delicious change. **MAKES ABOUT 3 CUPS**

FOR THE BEET SALAD

2 medium beets, halved

1 cup water

¼ cup chopped
fresh cilantro

¼ cup chopped
Spanish peanuts

1 teaspoon salt

¼ cup Greek yogurt, or more
as needed

FOR TEMPERING THE OIL

1 tablespoon peanut oil or
other high-smoke-point oil

¼ teaspoon mustard seeds

¼ teaspoon cumin seeds

½ teaspoon
ground turmeric

1. In the inner cooking pot of the Instant Pot®, place a trivet or steamer basket and arrange the beets in a single layer on the trivet. Pour in the water.

2. Lock the lid into place. Select Manual and adjust the pressure to High. Cook for 12 minutes.

3. When the cooking is complete, let the pressure release naturally. Unlock the lid and carefully remove the beets.

4. As soon as the beets are cool enough to handle, trim the tops and peel them. Dice them into ½-inch pieces and place in a medium bowl. Add the cilantro, peanuts, salt, and yogurt, and stir to combine. Add more yogurt if necessary to coat the beets.

TO TEMPER THE OIL

1. In a small saucepan over medium-high heat, add the oil. When it starts to shimmer, add the mustard seeds and cumin seeds. (If you don't have mustard seeds, double the amount of cumin seeds.) When the seeds start to sputter, remove the pan from the heat and add the turmeric. Stir, allowing the spices to cook and flavor the oil.

2. Carefully pour this hot oil over the chopped ingredients, and mix it all together. Taste and adjust the seasoning, adding more salt to taste.

3. Chill the salad in the refrigerator for at least 1 hour before serving.

Bundh Gobi Mutter CABBAGE AND PEAS

VEGAN

PREP TIME: 15 minutes

SAUTÉ: 7 minutes

MANUAL: 1 minute
high pressure

RELEASE: Quick

TOTAL TIME: 35 MINUTES

Bundh gobi mutter is a perfect two-for-one dish at our house. We eat it fresh and hot the first day, and later we eat it with yogurt mixed in as a cold salad, or koshimbir. This is definitely a tradition in our household. A delicious and unique blend of spicy and creamy, bundh gobi mutter may become a tradition at your house as well. **SERVES 4**

1 tablespoon peanut oil

¼ teaspoon cumin seeds

2 teaspoons minced garlic

1 teaspoon minced ginger

½ cup thinly sliced red onion

¼ teaspoon ground turmeric

3 cups chopped cabbage

¼ cup water

Salt

½ cup fresh or frozen green peas

Chopped fresh cilantro, for garnish

1. Preheat the Instant Pot® by selecting Sauté and adjusting to More for high heat. When the inner cooking pot is hot, add the oil and heat until it is shimmering. Add the cumin seeds and cook for about 1 minute, or until they start sputtering like popcorn popping.

2. Add the garlic and ginger. Let it all cook together for about 30 seconds. Add the onion and sauté until brown and crisp at the edges, about 5 minutes. Add the turmeric and let it mix into the oil.

3. Add the cabbage, water, and salt. Stir to combine.

4. Lock the lid into place. Select Manual and adjust the pressure to High. Cook for 1 minute.

5. When the cooking is complete, quick-release the pressure.

6. Add the peas and mix well to heat them through.

7. Garnish with the cilantro.

Tip: If you like your cabbage a little crunchy, try this with 0 minutes pressure, or cook on low pressure for 1 minute.

Baingan Bharta EGGPLANT WITH ONIONS

VEGETARIAN

PREP TIME: 15 minutes

MANUAL: 4 minutes
low pressure

SAUTÉ: 2 minutes

RELEASE: Natural
10 minutes, then Quick

TOTAL TIME: 40 MINUTES

Making baingan bharta the traditional way is a time-consuming process. An oiled and pierced eggplant is broiled in an oven or cooked on the stove top. Here, the eggplant gains its smoky taste by charring slices on high heat in the Instant Pot®. The 10 to 15 minutes you spend charring the vegetables will result in a smoky and flavorful melt-in-the-mouth bharta. Adjust the cayenne pepper up or down to suit your heat preference. **SERVES 4**

½ teaspoon peanut oil

1 small onion, thinly sliced

1 tomato, chopped

4 cups chopped eggplant

¼ teaspoon
ground turmeric

¼ teaspoon ground
cayenne pepper

¼ teaspoon Garam Masala
(page 24)

¼ teaspoon amchoor or
chaat masala (optional)

¼ teaspoon Goda Masala
(page 26) or chana
masala (optional)

¼ teaspoon salt

¼ cup heavy
(whipping) cream

1. In the inner cooking pot of the Instant Pot®, add the oil. Place the onion, tomato, and eggplant on top, in that order. You want the onion and tomato at the bottom to help create the moisture needed for this dish to cook, since you aren't adding any additional water.

2. Over the top of the vegetables, sprinkle the turmeric, cayenne, garam masala, amchoor (if using), goda masala (if using), and salt. Do not stir.

3. Lock the lid on the Instant Pot®. Select Manual and adjust the pressure to Low. Cook for 4 minutes.

4. When the cooking is complete, allow the pressure to release naturally for 10 minutes, then quick-release any remaining pressure.

5. Select Sauté and adjust to More for high heat. When the mixture starts to bubble, add the cream, stirring well to incorporate. Allow the cream to thicken a little, about 2 minutes, then serve.

Coconut-Tomato Soup

POUR AND COOK, VEGAN

PREP TIME: 10 minutes

MANUAL: 5 minutes
high pressure

RELEASE: Natural

TOTAL TIME: 40 MINUTES

Give tomato soup a zing with ginger and garlic, and expand its flavor with a luscious coconut finish. This soup begs you to throw everything into your Instant Pot® and walk away, and then return later to a nutritious, tasty soup the whole family will enjoy. **SERVES 4**

1 can coconut milk

1 red onion, diced

6 large tomatoes, cut into quarters

¼ cup chopped fresh cilantro

1 teaspoon minced garlic

1 teaspoon minced ginger

1 teaspoon salt

½ teaspoon ground cayenne pepper

1 teaspoon ground turmeric

1 tablespoon agave nectar or honey

1. In the inner cooking pot of the Instant Pot®, combine all of the ingredients.

2. Lock the lid into place. Select Manual and adjust the pressure to High. Cook for 5 minutes.

3. When the cooking is complete, let the pressure release naturally. Unlock the lid.

4. Using an immersion blender, mix the soup until smooth, and serve.

Marathi Kadhi TANGY YOGURT SOUP

VEGETARIAN

PREP TIME: 10 minutes

SAUTÉ: 1 minute

SOUP: 6 minutes
high pressure

RELEASE: Natural
10 minutes, then Quick

TOTAL TIME: 40 MINUTES

You have probably never had an Indian kadhi, unless you or someone you know is Indian. This recipe uses yogurt and chickpea flour (commonly called "besan" in Indian markets), resulting in a smooth, thick, tangy, spicy soup that goes well with rice. Punjabis add onions and fried vegetable fritters (pakodas) to theirs. Gujrathi kadhi is sweet and uses ginger-garlic paste. Sindhi kadhi is made with okra or eggplant. This kadhi, like me, is a mix of Punjabi and Marathi kadhi. It is delicious and quite unlike anything you will find in restaurants. Adjust the cayenne and chiles as desired for your spice preference. **SERVES 4**

1 cup full-fat yogurt (you can substitute soy yogurt)

2 cups water

1 teaspoon salt

1 teaspoon sugar

¼ teaspoon ground cayenne pepper

4 tablespoons chickpea flour

1 tablespoon Ghee (page 30) or coconut oil

1 teaspoon black mustard seeds

1 teaspoon cumin seeds

1 serrano chile, thinly sliced

1 tablespoon minced ginger

1 teaspoon ground turmeric

1. In a medium bowl, whisk together the yogurt, water, salt, sugar, cayenne, and chickpea flour until thoroughly mixed. (Don't let it get too frothy.) Set aside.

2. Preheat the Instant Pot® by selecting Sauté and adjusting to More for high heat. When the inner cooking pot is hot, add the ghee and heat until it is shimmering. Add the mustard seeds and cumin seeds and let them sputter for 10 to 20 seconds.

3. Add the serrano chile, ginger, and turmeric. Pour in the yogurt mixture and stir to combine.

4. Lock the lid into place. Select the Soup setting and adjust the pressure to High. Cook for 6 minutes.

5. When the cooking is complete, let the pressure release naturally for 10 minutes, then quick-release any remaining pressure. Unlock the lid, stir well, and serve with rice or a side of your choice.

Tip: I call for the Soup setting, as this function will not allow the yogurt to come to a vigorous boil.

Marathi Rassa MIXED VEGETABLES WITH COCONUT

VEGAN

PREP TIME: 15 minutes

SAUTÉ: 7 minutes

MANUAL: 3 minutes
low pressure

RELEASE: Quick

TOTAL TIME: 35 MINUTES

This Maharashtrian-style rassa is made by cooking whole vegetables with coconut and an excellent paste made from blended vegetables and herbs. While traditionally this is made using fresh coconut scraped from the shell, in this recipe I use unsweetened coconut flakes. Cut the vegetables into large chunks and do not overcook, or you may be making vegetable soup instead. Still, it would be a delectable vegetable soup! Add up to 1 teaspoon of cayenne pepper, if desired, to spice up the dish. **SERVES 6**

¼ cup unsweetened shredded coconut

½ cup hot water, divided, plus additional as needed

1 onion, chopped

2 tomatoes, chopped

4 garlic cloves, minced

1 tablespoon minced ginger

¼ cup chopped fresh cilantro

½ teaspoon ground cumin

½ teaspoon ground turmeric

¼ teaspoon ground cayenne pepper

1 teaspoon salt

1 tablespoon peanut oil

5 to 6 cups mixed vegetables, chopped into large pieces

1. In a blender jar or a food-processor bowl, add the coconut and cover it with ¼ cup of hot water. Let the coconut hydrate for about 10 minutes. (While it hydrates, you can prep the other ingredients.)

2. To the coconut, add the onion, tomatoes, garlic, ginger, cilantro, cumin, turmeric, cayenne, and salt. Process to a smooth purée. Add more water as necessary, but use as little as possible.

3. Preheat the Instant Pot® by selecting Sauté and adjusting to More for high heat. When the inner cooking pot is hot, add the oil and heat until it smokes slightly, then add the coconut-onion-tomato mixture.

4. Let the mixture cook, without stirring, until most of the water has evaporated, 3 to 5 minutes. At this point, stir continuously so that it cooks evenly and starts to lose its fresh green color, about another 2 minutes.

5. Add the chopped vegetables and the remaining ¼ cup of water and stir to combine.

6. Lock the lid into place. Select Manual and adjust the pressure to Low. Cook for 3 minutes.

7. When the cooking is complete, quick-release the pressure.

8. Unlock and remove the lid. Adjust the seasoning, adding more salt as necessary. Serve with naan, chapatis, or over rice.

Tip: Use any vegetables that cook quickly, such as cabbage, cauliflower, broccoli, carrots, potatoes, peas, squash, and corn.

Sindhi Sai Bhaji SINDHI-STYLE MIXED VEGETABLES

POUR AND COOK, VEGAN

PREP TIME: 10 minutes

MANUAL: 20 minutes
high pressure

RELEASE: Natural
10 minutes, then Quick

TOTAL TIME: 50 MINUTES

Here is a nice little vegan dish that involves throwing a bunch of nutritious things like dals and vegetables into your Instant Pot® and ending up with a lovely rich and thick soup. *Sai bhaji* means "green vegetables," but you can also try other versions that include okra and eggplant. Traditional recipes have you sauté the veggies to release the flavors, but with the Instant Pot®, the steps in the recipe are conveniently reduced. Use up to a whole chile, as desired, for your heat preference. **SERVES 8**

1 cup chopped tomato

1 cup chopped
butternut squash

1 cup chopped potato

¼ cup chana dal

¼ cup chopped fresh dill

5 garlic cloves, peeled

1 tablespoon minced ginger

½ to 1 jalapeño or other
green chile

1 teaspoon salt

1 teaspoon Garam Masala
(page 24)

½ teaspoon ground
turmeric

½ teaspoon
ground coriander

½ teaspoon ground cumin

¼ teaspoon ground
cayenne pepper

1 cup water

1. In the inner cooking pot of the Instant Pot®, combine all of the ingredients and stir.

2. Lock the lid into place. Select Manual and adjust the pressure to High. Cook for 20 minutes.

3. When the cooking is complete, let the pressure release naturally for 10 minutes, then quick-release any remaining pressure. Unlock and remove the lid.

4. Using an immersion blender, purée to create a smoother consistency, leaving some pieces intact for texture, and serve.

Paneer Biryani

PREP TIME: 10 minutes

SAUTÉ: 3 minutes

MANUAL: 5 minutes
high pressure

RELEASE: Natural

TOTAL TIME: 45 MINUTES

Adding paneer and vegetables in with the rice makes a delicious and easy one-pot meal for the family to enjoy. The flavorful rice combines well with the creamy paneer, and the vegetables add color and texture. You might be tempted to add more water to this recipe, but don't. What's called for is exactly enough. The resulting dish is gorgeous and colorful.

SERVES 6

2 tablespoons Ghee
(page 30) or peanut oil

1 small onion, thinly sliced

2 teaspoons minced ginger

4 garlic cloves, peeled
and crushed

2 jalapeños, diced

2 teaspoons Garam Masala
(page 24)

½ teaspoon salt

1 cup Paneer (page 32),
cut into cubes

1 cup frozen
mixed vegetables

½ cup chopped
fresh cilantro

6 to 8 fresh mint sprigs,
finely chopped

1 cup basmati rice, rinsed
and drained

1 cup water

1. Preheat the Instant Pot® by selecting Sauté and adjusting to More for high heat. When the inner cooking pot is hot, add the ghee, and heat until it is shimmering. Add the onion and cook until well browned. Add the ginger, garlic, and jalapeños, and cook for 2 to 3 minutes.

2. Add the garam masala and salt, and mix well. Keep in mind that you'll need enough salt to flavor the rice.

3. Add the paneer and the frozen vegetables, and spread them out to cover the bottom of the pot. Sprinkle the chopped cilantro and mint on top.

4. Spread the rinsed, drained rice across everything. Do not stir.

5. Pour in the water and gently push the rice down so it is mostly covered by the water.

6. Lock the lid into place. Select Manual and adjust the pressure to High. Cook for 5 minutes.

7. When the cooking is complete, let the pressure release naturally. Unlock the lid.

8. Open and inhale deeply! Enjoy the true-to-tradition aroma of this dish, and then either mix it gently from the bottom, or serve it by scooping up a layer from top to bottom so you include the paneer, vegetables, herbs, and rice in every serving.

Tip: If you have whole spices on hand, substitute them for the garam masala. To do this, after heating the oil in step 1, add ½ teaspoon of cumin seeds, 1 cinnamon stick, 3 or 4 whole cloves, 4 or 5 black peppercorns, and 4 or 5 green cardamom pods. Once the spices are sizzling, add the onion, ginger, garlic, and jalapeños, and follow the recipe from there as directed, omitting the garam masala.

Palak Paneer

VEGETARIAN

PREP TIME: 15 minutes

SAUTÉ: 1 minute

MANUAL: 4 minutes
high pressure

RELEASE: Quick

TOTAL TIME: 30 MINUTES

Palak paneer is one of the best-loved foods both inside and outside India. It's easy to make, and it's a recipe that allows you to throw the ingredients into your Instant Pot® and let the pot do all the work to make a fantastic and nourishing meal. With sautéed ginger and garlic to flavor the oil, the natural flavors of the spinach shine through. **SERVES 4**

2 teaspoons peanut oil

5 garlic cloves, chopped

2 teaspoons minced ginger

1 serrano or jalapeño chile, minced

1 pound fresh baby spinach

1 large yellow onion, chopped

2 medium tomatoes, chopped

2 teaspoons ground cumin

½ teaspoon ground cayenne pepper

2 teaspoons Garam Masala (page 24)

1 teaspoon ground turmeric

1 teaspoon salt

½ cup water

1½ cups Paneer (page 32), cut into ½-inch cubes

1. Preheat the Instant Pot® by selecting Sauté and adjust to More for high heat. When the inner cooking pot is hot, add the oil and heat until it is shimmering. Add the garlic, ginger, and chile, and sauté for 1 minute or until fragrant.

2. Add the spinach, onion, tomatoes, cumin, cayenne, garam masala, turmeric, salt, and water. Stir to combine.

3. Lock the lid into place. Select Manual and adjust the pressure to High. Cook for 4 minutes.

4. When the cooking is complete, quick-release the pressure. Unlock and remove the lid.

5. Using an immersion blender, purée the mixture to the consistency you prefer—either a very smooth purée or one with some bits left whole. You'll probably have to tilt the pot a little to get the blender to rotate properly.

6. Gently mix in the paneer, and serve.

CHICKEN TIKKA MASALA, PAGE 107

CHAPTER 5

Fish, Chicken & Meat

Patra ni Macchi FISH WITH GREEN CHUTNEY

PREP TIME: 15 minutes

MANUAL: 2 minutes
low pressure

RELEASE: Quick

TOTAL TIME: 25 MINUTES

This fish and chutney dish is a keeper because you use the chutney to coat the fish and flavor it while it is being steamed. Patra ni macchi is a classic dish often served at wedding feasts. But it's so easy to make, you definitely should not wait until your next wedding to try it. **SERVES 4**

1 pound tilapia fillets, (about 2 large fillets, or use other firm, white, mild fish)

½ cup Coconut Green Chutney (page 37)

1½ cups water

1. Cut the tilapia fillets in half. Cut 4 pieces of parchment paper each large enough to wrap one piece of fillet. Cut 4 pieces of aluminum foil each large enough to wrap a fish packet.

2. Place one piece of fish on a piece of parchment, and slather it with 2 tablespoons of green chutney, covering both sides. Wrap the fish in the parchment, and wrap the parchment packet with a piece of aluminum foil. Repeat with the remaining pieces of fish.

3. Into the inner cooking pot of the Instant Pot®, pour the water. Put in a trivet that will raise the fish above the water and place the fillet packets on the trivet.

4. Lock the lid into place. Select Manual and adjust the pressure to Low. Cook for 2 minutes. Use the quick method to release the pressure.

5. Unlock and remove the lid. Remove one packet of fish. Carefully unfold the packet to check the fish for doneness. If the fish is not quite done, put it back in the pot, close the lid, and let it steam with the cooker turned off, using the residual heat to finish cooking.

6. Serve with rice, naan, cauliflower rice, or something mild on the side.

Jhinga Nariyal Wala SHRIMP COCONUT CURRY

POUR AND COOK

PREP TIME: 10 minutes

MANUAL: 3 minutes
low pressure

RELEASE: Quick

TOTAL TIME: 25 MINUTES

The flavors in this curry are traditional and authentic. The dish was born of a need to put dinner on the table after a busy day. Indian dishes are often cooked in coconut milk, and many households make the milk from scratch. With canned coconut milk and a pound of shrimp, you can put this lovely coconut curry together in just a few minutes. A can opener, your spices, and an Instant Pot® are all you need. **SERVES 4**

1 pound shrimp, shelled and deveined (about 26 to 30 count)

1 tablespoon minced ginger

1 tablespoon minced garlic

½ teaspoon ground turmeric

1 teaspoon salt

½ teaspoon ground cayenne pepper

1 teaspoon Garam Masala (page 24)

1 cup unsweetened coconut milk, or more to taste

2 cups water

1. Place the shrimp in a bowl that fits inside the inner cooking pot of the Instant Pot®. Add the ginger, garlic, turmeric, salt, cayenne, garam masala, and coconut milk. Cover the bowl with foil.

2. Into the pot, pour the water, and place a trivet on top. Set the covered bowl on top of the trivet.

3. Lock the lid into place. Select Manual and adjust the pressure to Low. Cook for 3 minutes.

4. When the cooking is complete, use the quick method to release the pressure.

5. Unlock the lid. Add a little extra coconut milk if you like, stir well, and serve with rice or a side of your choice.

Tip: Eat with riced cauliflower, cucumber "noodles," or shirataki noodles for low-carb options, or over rice if carbs are not an issue.

Chicken Biryani

PREP TIME: 15 minutes

SAUTÉ: 5 minutes

MANUAL: 5 minutes
high pressure

RELEASE: Natural

TOTAL TIME: 50 MINUTES

I adore chicken biryani, but for decades I made it only for special occasions because of the amount of effort and time it required—so I needed to create a quick, convenient, and tasty recipe. After several tests, I produced a scrumptious chicken biryani that could be made without the time, effort, and dirty pots and pans. I now feel fulfilled, or at least full. This recipe calls for tempering whole spices, but you can eliminate that step by using garam masala. Jump to the tip for the instructions. **SERVES 6**

2 tablespoons Ghee (page 30) or butter

½ teaspoon cumin seeds

1 cinnamon stick

3 or 4 whole cloves

4 or 5 black peppercorns

4 or 5 green cardamom pods

1 small onion, thinly sliced

1 tablespoon minced ginger

4 garlic cloves, crushed

2 jalapeño chiles, diced

1 pound boneless, skinless chicken thighs, cut into bite-size pieces

½ cup chopped fresh cilantro

6 to 8 fresh mint sprigs, chopped fine

1 cup basmati rice, rinsed and drained

Salt

1 cup water

1. Preheat the Instant Pot® by selecting Sauté and adjust to More for high heat. When the inner cooking pot is hot, add the ghee and heat until it is shimmering. Add the cumin seeds, cinnamon, cloves, peppercorns, and cardamom pods. Stir and cook for 1 to 2 minutes, or until the spices are sizzling.

2. Once the spices sizzle, add the onion and cook until it's well browned and crisp at the edges.

3. Add the ginger, garlic, and jalapeños and cook for 2 to 3 minutes.

4. Add the chicken pieces and sear gently on both sides to precook the chicken slightly.

5. Spread out the chicken-and-vegetable mixture to cover the bottom of the pot.

6. Sprinkle the chopped cilantro and mint over the chicken mixture.

7. Spread the rice across everything and sprinkle salt over the top. Do not stir.

8. Pour in the water and gently push the rice down so it is mostly covered by the water.

9. Lock the lid into place. Select Manual and adjust the pressure to High. Cook for 5 minutes.

10. When the cooking is complete, let the pressure release naturally. Unlock the lid.

11. Open and inhale deeply! Enjoy the true-to-tradition aroma of this dish, and then either mix it gently from the bottom or serve it by scooping up a layer from top to bottom so you include the chicken, herbs, and rice in every serving.

Tip: If you don't have whole cinnamon, cardamom, cloves and peppercorn, use Garam Masala (page 24) and add it after you cook the chicken in step 4.

Murgh Makhani BUTTER CHICKEN

PREP TIME: 15 minutes

MANUAL: 10 minutes high pressure

SAUTÉ: 5 minutes

RELEASE: Natural

TOTAL TIME: 55 MINUTES

I spent years getting educated, received a PhD in psychology, and worked hard at becoming a scientist, an excellent statistician, and a top-flight marketing strategist. I never thought that I would be remembered in the Instant Pot® group as the "Butter Chicken Lady"! It makes me happy to hear about all the children who love the recipe, spouses that request it night after night, and especially Indian mothers-in-law who rave about it to their daughters-in-law. Perhaps my accomplishments could be combined, and I could be the "Dr. Butter Chicken Lady"? One practical note: This recipe makes twice as much sauce as you'll need. Believe me, make the full amount of sauce and save half to use on, well, everything else. **SERVES 4**

1 (14-ounce) can diced tomatoes (do not drain)

5 or 6 garlic cloves, minced

1 tablespoon minced ginger

1 teaspoon ground turmeric

1 teaspoon ground cayenne pepper

1 teaspoon ground paprika

2 teaspoons Garam Masala (page 24), divided

1 teaspoon ground cumin

1 teaspoon salt

1 pound boneless, skinless chicken (breasts or thighs)

4 ounces butter, cut into cubes, or ½ cup coconut oil

½ cup heavy (whipping) cream or full-fat coconut milk

¼ to ½ cup chopped fresh cilantro

1. In the inner cooking pot of the Instant Pot®, add the tomatoes, garlic, ginger, turmeric, cayenne, paprika, 1 teaspoon of garam masala, cumin, and salt. Mix thoroughly, then place the chicken pieces on top of the sauce.

2. Lock the lid into place. Select Manual and adjust the pressure to High. Cook for 10 minutes.

3. When the cooking is complete, let the pressure release naturally. Unlock the lid. Carefully remove the chicken and set it aside.

4. Using an immersion blender in the pot, blend together all the ingredients into a smooth sauce. Let the sauce cool for several minutes.

5. Add the butter cubes, cream, remaining 1 teaspoon of garam masala, and cilantro. Stir until well incorporated. The sauce should be thick enough to coat the back of a spoon when you're done.

6. Remove half of the sauce and freeze it for later, or refrigerate for up to 3 days.

7. Add the chicken back to the sauce. Preheat the Instant Pot® by selecting Sauté and adjust to Less for low heat. Let the chicken heat through. Break it up into smaller pieces if you like, but don't shred it.

8. Serve over rice or raw cucumber noodles.

Tip: It's incredibly easy to adapt this recipe to make a meatless version. Whether you want to replace the chicken with paneer, tofu, or vegetables, the only major change is that you'll need to add ¼ cup of water to the sauce before pressure cooking. Only after the sauce is cooked, add paneer or tofu, chopped to your preference. Vegetables should also be added after the sauce has cooked—just make sure you've steamed them first.

Punjabi Chicken Curry

PREP TIME: 15 minutes

SOUP: 8 minutes
high pressure

SAUTÉ: 5 minutes

RELEASE: Natural
10 minutes, then Quick

TOTAL TIME: 50 MINUTES

Cooking in yogurt adds a tangy taste to curry, and this combination of spicy, creamy, and tart gives this Punjabi chicken curry its distinctive flavor. A problem with this is that if cooked under pressure, the yogurt will separate. But this version uses the Soup button on the Instant Pot® to keep the yogurt together in a full-flavored, thick, and rich sauce. **SERVES 6**

1 onion, peeled
and quartered

2 tablespoons Ginger-
Garlic Paste (page 31)
(or 1 tablespoon each
minced ginger and garlic)

2 tomatoes, quartered

½ cup Greek Yogurt
(page 34)

2 tablespoons cornstarch

1 teaspoon salt

½ teaspoon ground
cayenne pepper

2 teaspoons
ground turmeric

2 teaspoons Garam Masala
(page 24), divided

¼ cup water

1½ pounds boneless,
skinless chicken thighs, cut
into large bite-size pieces

10 ounces fresh
spinach, chopped

1. In a food processor or blender, place the onion, ginger-garlic paste, tomatoes, yogurt, cornstarch, salt, cayenne, turmeric, 1 teaspoon of garam masala, and water. Blend until smooth.

2. In the inner cooking pot of the Instant Pot®, arrange the chicken. Pour in the sauce.

3. Lock the lid into place. Select Soup and adjust the pressure to High. Cook for 8 minutes.

4. When the cooking is complete, let the pressure release naturally for 10 minutes and then quick-release any remaining pressure.

5. Unlock and remove the lid. Remove the chicken to a cutting board.

6. Select Sauté and adjust for medium heat. Add the spinach to the sauce. When the chicken is cool enough to handle, cut it into smaller pieces, and add it back in. With the lid off, allow the sauce to simmer and thicken and the spinach to cook down.

7. Add the remaining 1 teaspoon of garam masala and stir.

8. Serve with rice, cauliflower rice, naan, or with mashed potatoes for a unique combination.

Tip: Though I call for bite-size pieces of chicken thighs, feel free to use your preferred cut of poultry in this recipe. Just make sure to adjust the cooking time per the cooking chart on page 145.

Chicken Vindaloo

PREP TIME: 15 minutes, plus up to 8 hours to marinate

COOK TIME: 7 minutes

MANUAL: 5 minutes high pressure

RELEASE: Natural 10 minutes, then Quick

TOTAL TIME: 50 MINUTES, PLUS TIME TO MARINATE

The Portuguese invasion of India left behind some culinary traces, the best known of which is probably the vindaloo, or the *vinha de alhos*, a technique of marinating meat with vinegar and spices. This popular dish comes from the western state of Goa, which was a Portuguese colony well into the twentieth century. While vindaloo has become synonymous with spice, homemade vindaloos need not be. Flavor emerges from other sources in this tangy, rich, and flavorful dish. Adjust the cayenne pepper to suit your spice preference. **SERVES 4**

1 cup diced onion

5 garlic cloves, minced

1 tablespoon minced ginger

1 tablespoon peanut oil

¼ cup white vinegar

1 cup chopped tomato

1 teaspoon salt

1 teaspoon Garam Masala (page 24)

1 teaspoon smoked paprika

½ teaspoon ground cayenne pepper

½ teaspoon ground coriander

½ teaspoon ground cumin

1 pound boneless, skinless chicken thighs

¼ cup water

½ teaspoon ground turmeric

1. In a large microwave-safe bowl, combine the onion, garlic, ginger, and oil. Heat in the microwave on full power for 5 to 7 minutes, until the vegetables are browned on the edges.

2. Transfer the onion mixture to a blender jar. Add the vinegar, tomato, salt, garam masala, paprika, cayenne, coriander, and cumin. Blend into a smooth paste.

3. Place the chicken in the bowl you used earlier, and spoon the spice-and-vegetable mix over it, mixing well to coat the chicken. Pour the water into the blender and pulse briefly to rinse out the remaining spices. Pour the spiced water over the chicken.

4. Add the turmeric and stir to combine (adding it earlier could stain your blender jar). Cover the bowl and marinate the chicken for 30 minutes or up to 8 hours. If you marinate it for longer than 30 minutes, cover and refrigerate the chicken.

5. Pour the chicken and marinade into the inner cooking pot of the Instant Pot®.

6. Lock the lid into place. Select Manual and adjust the pressure to High. Cook for 5 minutes.

7. When the cooking is complete, let the pressure release naturally for 10 minutes, then quick-release any remaining pressure.

8. Unlock and remove the lid.

9. If the sauce is too thin, select Sauté and adjust to More for high heat. Remove the chicken pieces and bring the sauce to a boil to evaporate some of the excess water. Return the chicken to the sauce and serve.

Chicken Korma

PREP TIME: 15 minutes

MANUAL: 10 minutes
high pressure

RELEASE: Natural

TOTAL TIME: 50 MINUTES

Korma, in the Urdu language, simply means "cooked meat." Because of the styles of restaurant cooking, korma is associated with a creamy, mild, and rich sauce. To increase the creaminess of this recipe, almonds are added, and then the dish is "finished" with a touch of coconut milk. A quick blending of the sauce ingredients followed by cooking under pressure in the Instant Pot® results in a dish that is rich, creamy, and flavorful, with a thick sauce that is not overly spicy.

FOR THE SAUCE

1 ounce raw almonds (or substitute cashews if you prefer)

1 small onion, chopped

½ cup diced tomato

½ green serrano chile

5 garlic cloves, peeled

1 tablespoon minced ginger

1 teaspoon ground turmeric

1 teaspoon salt

1 teaspoon Garam Masala (page 24)

1 teaspoon ground cumin

1 teaspoon ground coriander

½ teaspoon ground cayenne pepper

½ cup water

FOR THE KORMA

1 pound boneless, skinless chicken breasts, thighs, or drumsticks

½ cup full-fat coconut milk, or more to taste

1 teaspoon Garam Masala (page 24)

1 tablespoon tomato paste

¼ cup chopped fresh cilantro (optional)

FOR THE GARNISH

¼ cup slivered almonds

¼ cup chopped fresh cilantro

Pinch saffron strands, soaked in 2 tablespoons milk

Continued

TO MAKE THE SAUCE

In a blender jar, mix the almonds, onion, tomato, serrano, garlic, ginger, turmeric, salt, garam masala, cumin, coriander, cayenne, and water. Blend into a smooth purée.

TO MAKE THE KORMA

1. Pour the sauce into the inner cooking pot of the Instant Pot®. Place the chicken on top. If the chicken is frozen, push it down into the sauce a little.

2. Lock the lid into place. Select Manual and adjust the pressure to High. Cook for 10 minutes.

3. When the cooking is complete, let the pressure release naturally. Unlock and remove the lid.

4. Carefully remove the chicken to a board and cut it into bite-size pieces.

5. Stir the coconut milk, garam masala, and tomato paste into the pot. Return the chicken to the pot, and garnish with the slivered almonds and cilantro. Pour the saffron milk along with the saffron strands over the rice and serve.

Tip: It doesn't get any easier than this to make korma. You can add raisins and cashews for a sweeter flavor.

Chicken Tikka Masala

PREP TIME: 20 minutes, plus 1 to 2 hours to marinate

MANUAL: 10 minutes high pressure

RELEASE: Quick

TOTAL TIME: 40 MINUTES, PLUS TIME TO MARINATE

Did you know that chicken tikka masala is considered a national dish in Britain? While chicken tikka is definitely Indian, the sauce, or masala, that's added is a British manifestation. This curry is well loved inside and outside of India, and your Instant Pot® will allow you to make a wonderful version at home. **SERVES 6**

FOR THE MARINADE

½ cup Greek Yogurt (page 34)

4 garlic cloves, minced

2 teaspoons minced ginger

½ teaspoon ground turmeric

¼ teaspoon ground cayenne pepper

½ teaspoon smoked paprika

1 teaspoon salt

1 teaspoon Garam Masala (page 24)

½ teaspoon ground cumin

1 teaspoon liquid smoke (optional)

1½ pounds boneless, skinless chicken (breasts or thighs), cut into large pieces

FOR THE SAUCE

1 onion, chopped

1 (14-ounce) can diced tomatoes (do not drain)

1 carrot, chopped

5 garlic cloves, minced

2 teaspoons minced ginger

1 teaspoon ground turmeric

½ teaspoon ground cayenne pepper

1 teaspoon ground paprika

1 teaspoon salt

2 teaspoons Garam Masala (page 24)

1 teaspoon ground cumin

FOR FINISHING

½ cup half-and-half, heavy (whipping) cream, or full-fat coconut milk

1 teaspoon Garam Masala (page 24)

¼ to ½ cup chopped fresh cilantro

Continued

TO MAKE THE MARINADE

In a large bowl, mix together the yogurt, garlic, ginger, turmeric, cayenne, paprika, salt, garam masala, cumin, and liquid smoke (if using). Add the chicken and stir to coat. Marinate the chicken for 1 to 2 hours.

TO MAKE THE SAUCE

1. In the inner cooking pot of the Instant Pot®, mix the onion, tomatoes, carrot, garlic, ginger, turmeric, cayenne, paprika, salt, garam masala, and cumin. Place the chicken with the yogurt on top of the sauce ingredients.

2. Lock the lid into place. Select Manual and adjust the pressure to High. Cook for 10 minutes.

3. When the cooking is complete, use the quick method to release the pressure.

4. Unlock and remove the lid. Remove the chicken and set it aside. (If you like, you can brown it under the broiler or in an air fryer at this point.)

5. Using an immersion blender, purée the sauce well.

1. Add the half-and-half and the garam masala to the sauce, and stir well.

2. Remove half the sauce and freeze it for later.

3. Put the chicken back into the remaining sauce. Garnish with the cilantro and serve.

Tip: The spices for marinating and for the sauce are almost the same. To save time, you can add the marinade spices to a bowl and the sauce spices to the Instant Pot® at the same time.

Beef Curry

PREP TIME: 10 minutes

MANUAL: 20 minutes
high pressure

RELEASE: Natural

TOTAL TIME: 55 MINUTES

This is a proper—and versatile—curry, and you won't see store-bought curry powder listed in the ingredients. A true curry relies not on curry powder but on a good blend of spices. I love preparing a basic beef curry because the Instant Pot® intensifies all its wonderful flavors in just minutes, start to finish. Consider this a base curry recipe. You can easily swap the beef for chicken or lamb or pork; you need only to adjust the cooking time under pressure. **SERVES 4**

2 tomatoes,
cut into quarters

1 small onion,
cut into quarters

4 garlic cloves, peeled
and chopped

½ cup fresh cilantro

1 teaspoon ground cumin

½ teaspoon
ground coriander

1 teaspoon Garam Masala
(page 24)

½ teaspoon ground
cayenne pepper

1 teaspoon salt, plus more
for seasoning

1 pound beef chuck roast,
cut into 1-inch cubes

1. In a blender jar, combine the tomatoes, onion, garlic, and cilantro. (If you put the tomatoes at the bottom, they will liquefy first, and you won't have to add water.)

2. Process until all the vegetables have turned to a smooth purée.

3. Add the cumin, coriander, garam masala, cayenne, and salt. Process for several more seconds.

4. In the inner cooking pot of the Instant Pot®, add the beef and pour the vegetable purée on top.

5. Lock the lid into place. Select Manual and adjust the pressure to High. Cook for 20 minutes. Let the pressure release naturally.

6. Remove the lid and stir the curry. Taste and adjust, adding more salt if you like. Serve with naan.

Kheema Nariyal Saag
GROUND BEEF COCONUT CURRY AND SPINACH

PREP TIME: 15 minutes

SAUTÉ: 7 minutes

MANUAL: 10 minutes high pressure

RELEASE: Natural

TOTAL TIME: 60 MINUTES

If you grew up eating Indian food—either at home or in a restaurant—you're likely to have seen the word *saag* before. Any dish you add greens to is a saag, and typically it's spinach, as used here. This curry takes on an extra-rich flavor and thickness with the addition of coconut milk. Coconut milk tends to get a little thin when pressure cooked, so you add half at the beginning and save the other half to add after the dish is cooked. **SERVES 4**

1 tablespoon Ghee (page 30) or vegetable oil

2 teaspoons cumin seeds

4 tablespoons minced garlic

2 tablespoons minced ginger

1 pound ground beef

2 cups diced onion

1 cup chopped tomato

1 green serrano or jalapeño chile, minced

1 teaspoon ground turmeric

½ teaspoon ground cayenne pepper

1 teaspoon ground coriander

2 teaspoons Garam Masala (page 24)

2 teaspoons salt

4 cups chopped spinach, or more to taste

¼ cup water

1 (15-ounce) can coconut milk, divided

1. Preheat the Instant Pot® by selecting Sauté and adjust to More for high heat. When the inner cooking pot is hot, add the ghee.

2. When the ghee is shimmering, add the cumin seeds and cook until they sputter like popcorn popping, about 1 minute.

3. Add the garlic and ginger, and cook for 1 to 2 minutes or until they start to sizzle and flavor the oil.

4. Add the ground beef and cook, stirring occasionally, until the lumps have largely broken up, about 4 minutes.

5. Add the onion, tomato, chile, turmeric, cayenne, coriander, garam masala, salt, spinach, water, and half the can of coconut milk. Stir to combine.

6. Lock the lid into place. Select Manual and adjust the pressure to High. Cook for 10 minutes.

7. When the cooking is complete, let the pressure release naturally.

8. Unlock the lid and stir in the remaining half of the coconut milk to add thickness.

9. If you like, add more spinach and stir until it's wilted.

Kheema Matar SPICED GROUND BEEF

PREP TIME: 15 minutes

SAUTÉ: 10 minutes

MANUAL: 5 minutes
high pressure

RELEASE: Natural
10 minutes, then Quick

TOTAL TIME: 50 MINUTES

I love making this super hands-off Indian kheema. I'm not a fan of mixing sweet spices like cinnamon and cardamom with savory meats, but I made this low-carb, high-fat Indian kheema without the sweet spices, and it is just not the same. You don't taste the sweetness when eating it, just a wonderful complex flavor that will make it difficult to believe you spent less than 30 minutes cooking it. Adjust the cayenne to your spice preference as desired. **SERVES 4**

1 cup frozen peas

1 tablespoon Ghee (page 30) or peanut oil

3 or 4 cinnamon sticks

4 green or white cardamom pods

1 cup chopped onion

1 tablespoon minced garlic

1 tablespoon minced ginger

1 pound lean ground beef

1 teaspoon Garam Masala (page 24)

1 teaspoon salt

½ teaspoon ground turmeric

½ teaspoon ground cayenne pepper

½ teaspoon ground coriander

½ teaspoon ground cumin

¼ cup water

1. In a small bowl, measure out the peas and set them aside to thaw.

2. Preheat the Instant Pot® by selecting Sauté and adjusting to More for high heat. When the inner cooking pot is hot, add the ghee and heat until it is shimmering. Add the cinnamon sticks and cardamom and let them sizzle for 10 seconds.

3. Add the onion, garlic, and ginger and sauté for 3 to 5 minutes, until the onion has softened.

4. Add the ground beef and sauté long enough to break up the clumps, 3 to 4 minutes.

5. Add the garam masala, salt, turmeric, cayenne, coriander, cumin, and water.

6. Lock the lid into place. Select Manual and adjust the pressure to High. Cook for 5 minutes.

7. When the cooking is complete, let the pressure release naturally for 10 minutes, then quick-release any remaining pressure.

8. Unlock and remove the lid. Mix in the peas, let them heat through, and serve.

Pork Saag

PREP TIME: 10 minutes, plus up to 8 hours to marinate

SAUTÉ: 10 minutes

MANUAL: 10 minutes plus 2 minutes high pressure

RELEASE: Quick, then Natural

TOTAL TIME: 55 MINUTES, PLUS TIME TO MARINATE

This is a saag, which means that the pork is cooked with leafy greens. The only "difficult" thing about this recipe is remembering to marinate it ahead of time. The half-and-half marinade will help tenderize the pork. This will make a great quick and tasty weeknight summer meal if you can remember to plan ahead. **SERVES 4**

FOR THE MARINADE

⅓ cup half-and-half, plus more as needed

1 teaspoon minced garlic

½ teaspoon ground turmeric

½ teaspoon ground cayenne pepper

2 teaspoons Garam Masala (page 24)

1 teaspoon salt

1 pound pork shoulder, cut into bite-size cubes

FOR FINISHING THE PORK SAAG

1 tablespoon Ghee (page 30) or peanut oil

1 tablespoon tomato paste

¾ cup water

5 ounces fresh baby spinach, chopped

Salt

TO MAKE THE MARINADE

In a large bowl, mix the half-and-half, garlic, turmeric, cayenne, garam masala, and salt. Add the pork and stir to coat. Marinate the pork for at least 30 minutes or up to 8 hours. If you marinate for more than 30 minutes, cover and refrigerate the bowl until ready for use.

1. Preheat the Instant Pot® by selecting Sauté and adjust to More for high heat. When the inner cooking pot is hot, add the ghee and heat until it is shimmering. Add the pork along with the marinade and the tomato paste. Cook for 5 to 10 minutes or until the pork is lightly seared and the tomato paste has been well incorporated. Pour in the water.

2. Lock the lid into place. Select Manual and adjust the pressure to High. Cook for 10 minutes.

3. When the cooking is complete, quick-release the pressure. Carefully remove the lid and add the spinach. Mix well to incorporate.

4. Lock the lid into place. Select Manual and adjust the pressure to High. Cook for 2 minutes. Allow the pressure to release naturally.

5. Mix well and adjust the seasoning, adding more salt and half-and-half if desired.

Tip: This recipe can be made with any type of meat. Just use the half-and-half mixture to marinate it first.

Lamb Rogan Josh LAMB CURRY

PREP TIME: 10 minutes, plus up to 24 hours to marinate

MANUAL: 20 minutes high pressure

RELEASE: Natural

TOTAL TIME: 55 MINUTES, PLUS TIME TO MARINATE

Tender chunks of lamb smothered in a succulent sauce form the basis for this Kashmiri dish. Based on onion, yogurt, and tomato paste, the sauce combines a medley of complex spices with a smidgen of heat and flavor from paprika and cayenne pepper. Perhaps rogan josh is one of the reasons Kashmir is often described as paradise on Earth! SERVES 4

1 cup diced onion

2 teaspoons minced garlic

1 teaspoon minced ginger

¼ cup Greek Yogurt (page 34)

2 tablespoons tomato paste

1 teaspoon paprika

1 teaspoon Garam Masala (page 24)

1 teaspoon salt

½ teaspoon ground turmeric

½ teaspoon ground cinnamon

¼ teaspoon ground nutmeg

¼ teaspoon ground cayenne pepper

¼ cup water

1 pound boneless leg of lamb, cut into 1-inch cubes

1. In a large bowl, mix all of the ingredients except the lamb. Add the lamb and stir to coat. Cover the bowl and marinate in the refrigerator for 1 hour or up to 24 hours. (If pressed for time, skip marinating and proceed to cooking.)

2. Transfer the lamb mixture to the inner cooking pot of the Instant Pot®. Lock the lid into place. Select Manual and adjust the pressure to High. Cook for 20 minutes (15 minutes if you prefer chewier meat).

3. When the cooking is complete, let the pressure release naturally. Unlock the lid and serve.

Lamb Dum Biryani LAMB AND RICE CASSEROLE

PREP TIME: 20 minutes, plus
30 minutes to marinate

COOK TIME: 15 minutes

MANUAL: 6 minutes
high pressure

RELEASE: Natural

TOTAL TIME: 1 HOUR 5 MINUTES,
PLUS TIME TO MARINATE

A well sealed and slowly cooked dish is referred to as a *dum pukht*. Cooking a dum biryani with raw lamb at the bottom of the pot and rice on top is more akin to an art than a cooking method. It took several tries for me to get it right. The Instant Pot®, with its sealed environment, allows you to make a proper dum biryani without burning the lamb. The slow natural pressure release approximates the "dum" (steam cooking) part of the recipe. Here, I call for a longer list of ingredients than I usually advocate, but I assure you it is absolutely worth it. **SERVES 6**

1 cup basmati rice

½ cup Greek Yogurt
(page 34)

½ cup minced onion

½ cup chopped
fresh cilantro

¼ cup chopped fresh mint

1 tablespoon minced ginger

1 tablespoon minced garlic

2 teaspoons Garam Masala
(page 24)

1¾ teaspoons salt, divided

1 teaspoon ground turmeric

¼ teaspoon ground
cayenne pepper

¼ teaspoon
ground cardamom

¼ teaspoon
ground cinnamon

⅛ teaspoon ground cloves

1 serrano pepper, seeded
and minced

1 pound boneless shoulder
or leg of lamb, cut into
cubes and all visible
fat removed

1 onion, thinly sliced

1 teaspoon peanut oil

1 cup water

½ cup chopped
fresh cilantro

Continued

1. Rinse the rice and set it aside. This will allow the rice to soften a bit and absorb some water.

2. In a large bowl, mix together the yogurt, onion, cilantro, mint, ginger, garlic, garam masala, 1 teaspoon of salt, turmeric, cayenne, cardamom, cinnamon, cloves, and serrano pepper. Add the lamb and stir to coat the lamb cubes with the marinade. Let the lamb marinate for 30 minutes.

3. Preheat the oven to broil. Line a baking pan with aluminum foil.

4. With your fingers, break apart the onion slices onto the foil-lined pan. Add the remaining ¾ teaspoon of salt and the peanut oil, and mix well.

5. Broil the onions for about 15 minutes, stirring once or twice, until they are well browned and crisp. (Traditionally this is done in a pan on the stove, but it's quite a painstaking process. This method is largely hands-off and works well.) Set aside.

6. When the lamb has finished marinating, pour the marinade, along with the lamb, into the inner cooking pot of the Instant Pot®. Spread the lamb, yogurt, and spice mixture to cover the bottom of the pot.

7. Carefully spread the rice over all the meat in a uniform layer.

8. Pour in the water and gently push down the rice until it's submerged under the water. Do not mix the lamb and the rice together.

9. Lock the lid into place. Select Manual and adjust the pressure to High. Cook for 6 minutes.

10. When the cooking is complete, let the pressure release naturally.

11. Unlock the lid and serve, topped with the browned onions and cilantro.

Tip: Substitute beef or pork if you like, changing only the cooking time under pressure. For the best flavor, use aged Indian basmati, not an American basmati, if possible.

GAJJAR HALVA, PAGE 134

CHAPTER 6

Drinks & Desserts

Aam Panha RAW MANGO DRINK

VEGAN

PREP TIME: 10 minutes

MANUAL: 15 minutes
high pressure

RELEASE: Natural

TOTAL TIME: 50 MINUTES

If you are familiar with this drink, it can only be because you are Maharashtrian or Gujrathi, you know someone who is, or you grew up in India. You won't find it in a restaurant outside of India. This lovely and unusual drink is delicious and refreshing. What follows can only loosely be called a recipe. Because raw mangos vary in tartness as well as pulp, this is similar to making fresh lemonade. You add, you taste, you add some more, and taste again (and repeat as necessary). **SERVES 4**

1 green mango (unripe and hard)

4¼ cups water, divided, plus more as needed

⅓ cup sugar or brown sugar

1 teaspoon ground cardamom, or more to taste

½ cup ice cubes

1. Slice the whole raw mango lengthwise into 3 pieces (one will be the large seed) and transfer it to a heat-proof bowl that fits into the inner cooking pot of the Instant Pot®. Pour in ¼ cup of water. Cover tightly with aluminum foil.

2. Into the inner cooking pot of the Instant Pot®, pour 2 cups of water and place a trivet in the liner. Place the bowl on the trivet.

3. Lock the lid into place. Select Manual and adjust the pressure to High. Cook for 15 minutes.

4. When the cooking is complete, let the pressure release naturally.

5. Unlock and remove the lid. Check to see if the mango is soft and pulpy; if not, cook again for a few more minutes.

6. Once the mango is cool, pull off the peel and get ready to get messy (or better still, ask your kids to help). Squeeze all the pulp you can off the peel and the seed. Save whatever cooking water remains in the bowl.

7. Push the pulp and water through a wire-mesh strainer, being sure to get all the last little bits. It should yield about 1 cup of purée.

8. Add the sugar and cardamom, and stir well until the sweetener is completely dissolved. Stir in the remaining 2 cups of water plus the ice. Taste, adjusting the sugar and adding more cardamom as desired.

9. Serve in small cups as a dessert drink, or dilute more and serve as "mango-ade."

Gulabi Doodh ROSE MILK

VEGETARIAN

PREP TIME: 5 minutes

MANUAL: 4 minutes
high pressure

RELEASE: Natural

TOTAL TIME: 35 MINUTES

Tip: Dried culinary rose petals can be found in some international markets or online. You can use rose petals from your garden, or a neighbor's, but be sure they are pesticide-free.

This lightly rose-flavored milk is a wonderful, exotic way to cool off during the summer—or drink it hot to warm yourself up during the winter. *Gulab* is the Hindi word for "rose." I created this recipe to use up some leftover rose petals, and it was worth every petal. To make it even more of a treat, add a dollop of whipped cream to each serving. **SERVES 6**

¼ cup raw cashews

2 cups whole milk (or substitute nondairy milk)

¼ cup dried rose petals

1 tablespoon sugar or honey

4 drops red food coloring (optional)

2 cups water

1. In a heatproof bowl that fits into the inner cooking pot of the Instant Pot®, combine the cashews, milk, rose petals, sugar, and food coloring (if using). Cover the bowl with aluminum foil.

2. Into the pot, pour the water, and place a trivet in the bottom. Place the foil-covered bowl on the trivet.

3. Lock the lid into place. Select Manual and adjust the pressure to High. Cook for 4 minutes.

4. When the cooking is complete, let the pressure release naturally. The slower release time allows a fuller infusion of the flavor into the milk.

5. When the milk is sufficiently cooled, pour it into a blender and purée until smooth. Chill.

6. Serve chilled in small cups.

Masala Chai SPICED TEA

VEGETARIAN

PREP TIME: 5 minutes

MANUAL: 4 minutes
high pressure

RELEASE: Natural
5 minutes, then Quick

TOTAL TIME: 25 MINUTES

Chai means "tea," so now you know why it's actually not necessary to ask for a "chai tea" next time you go to Starbucks. This version is a strong and authentic Indian masala chai. We call it "kadak chai," or "strong tea." We drink cup upon cup upon cup of this chai all day long. It tastes much like tea, with a pleasant back flavor of spices. Try it as written first, then adjust the spices to suit your taste buds. **SERVES 2**

2 or 3 tea bags

1½ cups water

½ cup milk or nondairy substitute

2 teaspoons sugar or honey

2 whole cloves

3 or 4 cinnamon sticks

1 tablespoon minced ginger

½ teaspoon fennel seeds

4 green cardamom pods

1. In a heatproof container that fits into the inner cooking pot of the Instant Pot® (preferably one with a spout to ease pouring), combine all the ingredients. Cover the container with aluminum foil.

2. Into the pot, pour 2 cups of water, and place a trivet in the bottom. Place the foil-covered bowl on the trivet.

3. Lock the lid into place. Select Manual and adjust the pressure to High. Cook for 4 minutes.

4. When the cooking is complete, let the pressure release naturally for 5 minutes, then quick-release any remaining pressure.

5. Strain into 2 cups and serve.

Caramel Custard

VEGETARIAN

PREP TIME: 25 minutes

SAUTÉ: 22 minutes

TOTAL TIME: 50 MINUTES,
PLUS 4 HOURS TO CHILL

You're probably wondering why this recipe is in an Indian cookbook. This is actually a very popular dessert in India, no doubt a result of the British influence on the country. It's easy to make, and yet it looks so elegant. This custard is quite different from a flan. It's not as sweet or as dense. It's a light, flavor-packed, scrumptious little morsel. It has both eggs and milk, so you can eat it as breakfast and tell yourself it's perfectly okay and healthy. Although it doesn't cook under pressure, it requires a hot, steamy environment to cook into a smooth, creamy custard. The Instant Pot® does a fine job of providing just such an environment. **SERVES 6**

5 tablespoons sugar	2 cups whole milk
2 cups plus 2 tablespoons water	¼ cup sugar or other sweetener
3 eggs	½ teaspoon vanilla extract

1. In a small pot, heat the sugar and 2 tablespoons of water over medium-high heat. Stir occasionally until the water boils, but once it starts boiling, do not stir. Continue to cook until the liquid is caramel in color and thickened. Being careful with the hot mixture, pour it into a 6-inch soufflé dish that fits inside the inner cooking pot of the Instant Pot®.

2. In a mixing bowl, whisk together the eggs, milk, sugar, and vanilla.

3. Pour this custard mixture through a strainer onto the top of the hardened caramel in the soufflé dish. Cover the dish with aluminum foil.

4. Pour the remaining 2 cups of water into the inner cooking pot, and place a trivet in the bottom. Place the dish on the trivet. Lock the lid into place and set the pressure release valve to Venting (you won't be pressure cooking this).

5. Select Sauté and adjust to More for high heat. Set a timer for 22 minutes. (Remember, since you're not using the pressure-cooking function, the cooker will not serve as a timer.)

6. When the timer goes off, turn off the pot and carefully open the lid. Insert a toothpick into the center of the custard to check for doneness. The center will be jiggly, but the toothpick should come out clean. If not, turn the Instant Pot® back to Sauté and cover it with the lid. Cook for another 2 to 3 minutes or as necessary until it is set.

7. Refrigerate for 4 to 6 hours or until well chilled.

8. When the custard is ready to serve, use a knife to loosen the edges, place a plate on top of the dish, and invert it. Thump the bottom of the dish to help it along if needed. The custard should unmold easily.

Elaichi Dahi CREAMY CARDAMOM YOGURT

PREP TIME: 15 minutes

YOGURT: 8 hours

TOTAL TIME: 8 HOURS
15 MINUTES, PLUS 6 HOURS
TO CHILL

This base recipe for a smooth and creamy yogurt can be adapted to your spice preference. It's a perfect beginner's recipe, as the gelatin in the yogurt helps it set. You can substitute your choice of sweetener. The creamy texture will appeal to picky eaters who are used to overly sweet store-bought yogurts. Once you have the process down, try swapping the cardamom for apple pie spice, pumpkin spice, or cinnamon for variety. **SERVES 8**

2 cups whole milk, divided

½ cup heavy (whipping) cream

1½ teaspoons unflavored gelatin

2 to 3 tablespoons plain unsweetened yogurt (any type with live cultures)

½ teaspoon ground cardamom

5 tablespoons sugar or honey

1½ teaspoons honey, plus more as needed (optional)

1. In a microwave-safe bowl, heat the milk and cream in the microwave for 2 minutes. Using a thermometer, make sure the temperature is between 98°F and 110°F.

2. In a small bowl, put ¼ cup of the warm milk in the gelatin and mix until smooth, then add this mixture to the milk and cream.

3. Add the starter yogurt, sugar (or honey), and cardamom and whisk until everything is well incorporated. Pour the yogurt into 8 to 10 small (6-ounce) glass jars and twist on the lids.

4. On the Instant Pot®, select Yogurt and set the timer to 8 hours. Place a trivet on the bottom of the inner cooking pot, and place the jars on the trivet.

5. Once the Yogurt cycle is done, take out the jars, stir the yogurt, and add the honey (if using). Taste for sweetness and adjust as desired.

6. Place the jars in the refrigerator and let them chill for 6 to 8 hours so the gelatin has a chance to set.

Tip: You can either buy powdered cardamom, buy the seeds and grind them yourself in a coffee grinder, or peel the green cardamom pods, remove the seeds, and then grind those. I buy seeds and grind them fresh each time.

Mitha Dahi STEAMED YOGURT CUSTARD

POUR AND COOK, VEGETARIAN

PREP TIME: 5 minutes

MANUAL: 20 minutes
high pressure

RELEASE: Natural
10 minutes, then Quick

TOTAL TIME: 45 MINUTES

Sometimes when you're creating new recipes, you come up with something that your family labels "outrageously delicious," but you don't really know what to call it. This is one. It's simple to make, but the result is a sweet, creamy, slightly grainy dessert that is flavored with lots of cardamom. **SERVES 6**

1 cup Greek Yogurt
(page 34)

1 cup sweetened
condensed milk

1 cup whole milk

2 teaspoons
ground cardamom

2 cups water

1. In a heatproof bowl that fits into the inner cooking pot of the Instant Pot®, mix together the yogurt, condensed milk, whole milk, and cardamom. Cover the bowl with aluminum foil.

2. Into the pot, pour the water, and place a trivet in the bottom. Place the foil-covered bowl on the trivet.

3. Lock the lid into place. Select Manual and adjust the pressure to High. Cook for 20 minutes.

4. When the cooking is complete, let the pressure release naturally for 10 minutes, then quick-release any remaining pressure.

5. Unlock and remove the lid. Carefully remove the bowl from the inner pot and test the custard. A knife inserted into the custard should emerge clean. If it is not cooked through, cover and place it back into the pot to cook in the residual heat for 1 or 2 minutes longer until finished.

6. Refrigerate the dessert until well chilled.

A Maharashtrian Specialty

SHRIKHAND WITH GREEK YOGURT

**SERVES 4 / PREP TIME: 15 MINUTES,
PLUS 4 TO 6 HOURS TO CHILL**

I've always had a bit of a love/don't love (never hate) relationship with shrikhand, a uniquely Maharashtrian dessert. As a child, I thought it was my grandmother feeding me yogurt and lying to me about it being a dessert. As an adult, I've come to appreciate the mix of the tangy yogurt, the sweetness that offsets the tang, and the wonderful aromas of cardamom and saffron that permeate this delicious dessert. This is a simple, no-cook dessert, but you do need to chill it for 4 to 6 hours for the best results.

Pinch saffron
2 tablespoons hot water
2 cups Greek Yogurt (page 34)
½ cup powdered sugar
¼ to ½ teaspoon ground cardamom

1. In a small bowl, stir together the saffron and hot water. Set aside for 5 to 10 minutes to soften the saffron and color the water.

2. Meanwhile, in a medium bowl, mix together the yogurt, sugar, and cardamom. Taste and adjust for sweetness. The first thing you taste should be sweet. The tang of the yogurt should be the end taste, not the first taste.

3. Pour in the softened saffron and the water and mix again. Mash up the saffron well to extract the flavor and color.

4. Refrigerate for 4 to 6 hours, stirring from time to time, to get as much flavor and color as you can from the saffron. You'll notice that each time you stir, you get a little more color. You don't need to be compulsive about this; just whenever you remember, give it a stir. Once the dessert has a lovely light orange-yellow hue and is chilled, it's done.

Gajjar Halva CARROT WITH RAISINS

VEGETARIAN

PREP TIME: 10 minutes

SAUTÉ: 4 minutes

MANUAL: 10 minutes
high pressure

RELEASE: Natural

TOTAL TIME: 50 MINUTES

This popular carrot dessert is usually made with khoya, which is milk solids with all the water evaporated away. But making khoya takes all day and requires standing over it and stirring so the milk doesn't burn. This much simpler version involves pressure-cooking to separate the milk, and creating milk solids quickly that get mixed back into the halva to re-create the traditional taste without the all-day labor. Grind the cashews to powder in a clean spice grinder before you get started to make it all come together quickly. **SERVES 6**

2 tablespoons Ghee
(page 30)

2 tablespoons raw cashews

2 tablespoons raisins

2 cups shredded carrots

1 cup whole milk

¼ cup sugar or
other sweetener

2 tablespoons ground
cashews (to thicken
the milk)

¼ teaspoon
ground cardamom

Chopped pistachios,
for garnish

1. Preheat the Instant Pot® by selecting Sauté and adjust to More for high heat. When the inner cooking pot is hot, add the ghee and heat until it shimmers. Add the whole cashews and raisins and cook them until the cashews are golden brown, about 4 minutes.

2. Add the carrots, milk, sugar, and ground cashews, and stir to combine.

3. Lock the lid into place. Select Manual and adjust the pressure to High. Cook for 10 minutes.

4. When the cooking is complete, let the pressure release naturally. Unlock and open the lid.

5. The mixture will look curdled, but don't worry. Stir well, mashing the carrots together a bit. Select Sauté and cook, stirring, for a few minutes to thicken the mixture.

6. Turn the pot off by selecting Cancel. Stir in the cardamom and let the mixture rest for 10 minutes to thicken up. Garnish with the pistachios before serving. This dessert can be eaten hot, cold, or at room temperature.

Tip: Feel free to pour in a little heavy (whipping) cream or half-and-half if you're trying to add fat to your diet—or taste to your life.

Chawal Ki Kheer INDIAN RICE PUDDING

VEGETARIAN

PREP TIME: 10 minutes

SAUTÉ: 4 minutes

MANUAL: 15 minutes
high pressure

RELEASE: Natural

**TOTAL TIME: 55 MINUTES,
PLUS OVERNIGHT TO CHILL**

Although Indian restaurants routinely serve up a white-rice kheer, it can sometimes be a little mediocre. Proper kheer should be thick, slightly caramelized, and rosy pink. The trick to making smooth, creamy, caramelized kheer is to cook it until the milk separates, and then to stir the milk solids back into the final dish. Don't be alarmed when you see the separated milk. Just stir everything up from the bottom, add more milk, stir again, and enjoy the caramelized goodness. **SERVES 6**

2 tablespoons Ghee
(page 30)

¼ cup raisins

¼ cup cashews

¼ cup basmati rice, rinsed

2 cups whole milk

¼ cup sugar

½ cup water

½ cup half-and-half

¼ to ½ teaspoon
ground cardamom

1. Preheat the Instant Pot® by selecting Sauté and adjust to More for high heat. When the inner cooking pot is hot, add the ghee and heat until it shimmers. Add the raisins and cashews. Stir and cook until the cashews are lightly browned and the raisins are plumped, about 4 minutes. Add the rice, milk, sugar, and water.

2. Lock the lid into place. Select Manual and adjust the pressure to High. Cook for 15 minutes.

3. When the cooking is complete, let the pressure release naturally. Unlock and remove the lid.

4. Stir until the contents are well mixed, adding the half-and-half a little at a time to thin it out. Don't worry about the curdled milk. By this time, you will have a smooth, noncurdled kheer.

5. Stir in the cardamom, pour the mixture into a bowl, and chill overnight. (You can eat it hot, but really it's so much better the next day.)

Narali Bhat SWEET COCONUT RICE

VEGAN

PREP TIME: 10 minutes

RICE: 12 minutes
low pressure

RELEASE: Natural

TOTAL TIME: 45 MINUTES,
PLUS OVERNIGHT TO CHILL

Coastal Maharashtra, with its easy access to coconut, has devised ways to include coconut in both savory and sweet dishes. This dish is typically made for a festival called Narali Poornima, which is at a full moon that marks the transition between the end of the rainy season and the beginning of the fishing season, when it is safe for fishermen to go out to sea and resume their trade. This sweet rice dish acts as a little bit of dessert, but it is served along with the rest of the meal. My one-step recipe asks you to place all the ingredients into your Instant Pot®, and allows pressure-cooking to extract all the flavor from the coconut, creating its own sugar syrup as the rice cooks. This makes it a fast, easy dessert. Note that the flavorful whole spices—cinnamon and cardamom pods—cook right along with everything else, but you'll want to eat around them when the rice is finished. **SERVES 4**

½ cup unsweetened shredded coconut

½ cup hot water

1 cup jasmine rice, rinsed and drained

½ cup brown sugar or palm sugar

¼ cup raisins

2 teaspoons Ghee (page 30)

Pinch saffron

4 whole cloves

1 cinnamon stick, cut into 3 or 4 pieces

4 green cardamom pods

½ teaspoon ground cardamom

1. In a small bowl, combine the coconut and hot water.

2. In the inner cooking pot of the Instant Pot®, add the rice, sugar, raisins, ghee, saffron, cloves, cinnamon, and cardamom pods.

3. Drain the coconut and add it to the rice.

4. Lock the lid into place. Select the Rice setting (it should default to low pressure and cook for 12 minutes).

5. When the cooking is complete, let the pressure release naturally.

6. Unlock and remove the lid. Stir in the ground cardamom.

7. Serve as a sweet side dish or as a dessert.

Instant Pot® Pressure Cooking Time Charts

The following charts provide approximate times for a variety of foods. To begin, you may want to cook for a minute or two less than the times listed; you can always simmer foods at natural pressure to finish cooking.

Keep in mind that these times are for foods partially submerged in water (or broth) or steamed, and for foods cooked alone. Depending on the recipe, the same foods may have different cooking times because of the use of additional ingredients, the presence of cooking liquids, or the direction for a different release method than the one listed below.

For any foods labeled with "Natural" release, allow at least 15 minutes of natural pressure release before quick-releasing any remaining pressure.

BEANS AND LEGUMES

When cooking beans, if you have a pound or more, it's best to use low pressure and increase the cooking time by a minute or two (with larger amounts, there's more chance for foaming at high pressure). If you have less than a pound, high pressure is fine. A little oil in the cooking liquid will reduce foaming.

Unless a shorter release time is indicated, let the beans release naturally for at least 15 minutes, after which any remaining pressure can be quick-released.

	MINUTES UNDER PRESSURE (Unsoaked)	MINUTES UNDER PRESSURE (Soaked in salted water)	PRESSURE	RELEASE
Black beans	22	10	High	Natural
	25	12	Low	
Black-eyed peas	12	5	High	Natural for 8 minutes, then quick
	15	7	Low	
Cannellini beans	25	8	High	Natural
	28	10	Low	
Chickpeas (garbanzo beans)	18	3	High	Natural for 3 minutes, then quick
	20	4	Low	
Kidney beans	25	8	High	Natural
	28	10	Low	
Lentils	10	not recommended	High	Quick
Lima beans	15	4	High	Natural for 5 minutes, then quick
	18	5	Low	
Navy beans	18	8	High	Natural
	20	10	Low	
Pinto beans	25	10	High	Natural
	28	12	Low	
Split peas (unsoaked)	5 (firm peas) to 8 (soft peas)	not recommended	High	Natural
Soy beans, fresh (edamame)	1	not recommended	High	Quick
Soybeans, dried	25	12	High	Natural
	28	14	Low	

GRAINS

To prevent foaming, it's best to rinse these grains thoroughly before cooking, or include a small amount of butter or oil with the cooking liquid.

	LIQUID PER 1 CUP OF GRAINS	MINUTES UNDER PRESSURE	PRESSURE	RELEASE
Arborio (or other medium-grain) rice	1½ cups	6	High	Quick
Barley, pearled	2½ cups	10	High	Natural
Brown rice, medium-grain	1½ cups	6–8	High	Natural
Brown rice, long-grain	1½ cups	13	High	Natural for 10 minutes, then quick
Buckwheat	1¾ cups	2–4	High	Natural
Farro, pearled	2 cups	6–8	High	Natural
Farro, whole-grain	3 cups	22–24	High	Natural
Oats, rolled	3 cups	3–4	High	Quick
Oats, steel-cut	4 cups	12	High	Natural
Quinoa	2 cups	2	High	Quick
Wheat berries	2 cups	30	High	Natural for 10 minutes, then quick
White rice, long-grain	1½ cups	3	High	Quick
Wild rice	2½ cups	18–20	High	Natural

MEAT

Except when noted, these times are for braised meats—that is, meats that are seared before pressure cooking and partially submerged in liquid.

	MINUTES UNDER PRESSURE	PRESSURE	RELEASE
Beef, bone-in short ribs	40	High	Natural
Beef, flat iron steak, cut into ½" strips	1	Low	Quick
Beef, sirloin steak, cut into ½" strips	1	Low	Quick
Beef, shoulder (chuck) roast (2 lb)	35	High	Natural
Beef, shoulder (chuck), 2" chunks	20	High	Natural for 10 minutes
Lamb, shanks	35–40	High	Natural
Lamb, shoulder, 2" chunks	15–20	High	Natural
Pork, shoulder roast (2 lb)	25	High	Natural
Pork, shoulder, 2" chunks	20	High	Natural
Pork, back ribs (steamed)	30	High	Quick
Pork, spare ribs (steamed)	20	High	Quick
Pork, smoked sausage, ½" slices	20	High	Quick
Pork, tenderloin	4	Low	Quick

POULTRY

Except when noted, these times are for braised poultry—that is, partially submerged in liquid.

	MINUTES UNDER PRESSURE	PRESSURE	RELEASE
Chicken breast, bone-in (steamed)	8	Low	Natural for 5 minutes
Chicken breast, boneless (steamed)	5	Low	Natural for 8 minutes
Chicken thigh, bone-in	15	High	Natural for 10 minutes
Chicken thigh, boneless	8	High	Natural for 10 minutes
Chicken thigh, boneless, 1"–2" pieces	5	High	Quick
Chicken, whole (seared on all sides)	12–14	Low	Natural for 8 minutes
Duck quarters, bone-in	35	High	Quick
Turkey breast, tenderloin (12 oz) (steamed)	5	Low	Natural for 8 minutes
Turkey thigh, bone-in	30	High	Natural

FISH AND SEAFOOD

All times are for steamed fish and shellfish.

	MINUTES UNDER PRESSURE	PRESSURE	RELEASE
Clams	2	High	Quick
Halibut, fresh (1" thick)	3	High	Quick
Mussels	1	High	Quick
Salmon, fresh (1" thick)	5	Low	Quick
Shrimp, large, frozen	1	Low	Quick
Tilapia or cod, fresh	1	Low	Quick
Tilapia or cod, frozen	3	Low	Quick

VEGETABLES

The cooking method for all the following vegetables is steaming; if the vegetables are cooked in liquid, the times may vary. Green vegetables will be tender-crisp; root vegetables will be soft.

	PREP	MINUTES UNDER PRESSURE	PRESSURE	RELEASE
Acorn squash	Halved	9	High	Quick
Artichokes, large	Whole	15	High	Quick
Beets	Quartered if large; halved if small	9	High	Natural
Broccoli	Cut into florets	1	Low	Quick
Brussels sprouts	Halved	2	High	Quick
Butternut squash	Peeled, ½" chunks	8	High	Quick
Cabbage	Sliced	5	High	Quick
Carrots	½"–1" slices	2	High	Quick
Cauliflower	Cut into florets	1	Low	Quick
Cauliflower	Whole	6	High	Quick
Green beans	Cut in half or thirds	1	Low	Quick
Potatoes, large, russet (for mashing)	Quartered	8	High	Natural for 8 minutes, then quick
Potatoes, red	Whole if less than 1½" across, halved if larger	4	High	Quick
Spaghetti squash	Halved lengthwise	7	High	Quick
Sweet potatoes	Halved lengthwise	8	High	Natural

Measurement Conversions

VOLUME EQUIVALENTS (LIQUID)

US STANDARD	US STANDARD (OUNCES)	METRIC (APPROXIMATE)
2 tablespoons	1 fl. oz.	30 mL
¼ cup	2 fl. oz.	60 mL
½ cup	4 fl. oz.	120 mL
1 cup	8 fl. oz.	240 mL
1½ cups	12 fl. oz.	355 mL
2 cups or 1 pint	16 fl. oz.	475 mL
4 cups or 1 quart	32 fl. oz.	1 L
1 gallon	128 fl. oz.	4 L

OVEN TEMPERATURES

FAHRENHEIT (F)	CELSIUS (C) (APPROXIMATE)
250°	120°
300°	150°
325°	165°
350°	180°
375°	190°
400°	200°
425°	220°
450°	230°

VOLUME EQUIVALENTS (DRY)

US STANDARD	METRIC (APPROXIMATE)
⅛ teaspoon	0.5 mL
¼ teaspoon	1 mL
½ teaspoon	2 mL
¾ teaspoon	4 mL
1 teaspoon	5 mL
1 tablespoon	15 mL
¼ cup	59 mL
⅓ cup	79 mL
½ cup	118 mL
⅔ cup	156 mL
¾ cup	177 mL
1 cup	235 mL
2 cups or 1 pint	475 mL
3 cups	700 mL
4 cups or 1 quart	1 L

WEIGHT EQUIVALENTS

US STANDARD	METRIC (APPROXIMATE)
½ ounce	15 g
1 ounce	30 g
2 ounces	60 g
4 ounces	115 g
8 ounces	225 g
12 ounces	340 g
16 ounces or 1 pound	455 g

Recipe Index

Index

Acknowledgments

All that we are, all that we become, all that we want to be is often made possible by those around us. In this, I have been particularly blessed.

My paternal grandmother, Indumati Pitre, taught me traditional Maharashtrian cuisine. A gentle, quiet soul, she also had the strength to intervene on behalf of my brother and me in those moments when we had driven every other grown-up around us to distraction. I admired her so very much—a fact I didn't realize until after she was gone. To her, I owe my love for, and heritage of, Maharashtrian cooking.

My mother, Veena Pitre, about whom I cannot say enough. A major in the Indian army, recipient of a distinguished service award, award-winning operation theater nurse, accomplished chef, beautician, teacher, healer, candle-maker, stuffed-toy maker, batik artist, and macramé and crotchet expert—and a woman who always found time for her family despite her busy schedule. She never stopped learning. She taught me so much and died so young, yet the near-legendary status she acquired among those who knew her lives on.

My husband, Roger Gorman, who puts up with me. I have so many things to be thankful to him for that I will confine myself to his role in this book. He tasted everything I made and gave me honest feedback. He's the reason I made butter chicken three times and narali bhat four times before they were deemed acceptable. He also took all the beautiful pictures on my blog and did his best to salvage the terrible pictures I took. Thank you, for all the times that you had to tell me that my latest creation was not up to snuff, and thank you for teaching me a little about photography, despite my best efforts to remain ignorant.

My son Alex, who is a picky eater but pitched in to taste these dishes to ensure that they weren't too spicy for little children. His encouragement and support has meant a lot to me. Most importantly, though, Alex, thanks for doing all the dishes and not complaining about it, even after some of my most epic cooking fails.

My son Mark, who has taught me so much. Mark first learned to cook with a pressure cooker, and the joy of the times when my son first produced authentic Indian cooking remains a cherished memory for me.

My heartfelt thanks to those who read my blog, read my posts, try my recipes, encourage me, provide feedback, and have urged me to write a cookbook. I would never have thought of it had it not been for all of you.

Thanks to the company behind the Instant Pot®, not only for producing a spectacular product and for authorizing this book, but for also creating a supportive and positive online community that helped me immeasurably.

About the Author

 *Urvashi Pitre* is a successful entrepreneur and the founder of Tasseologic, a data-driven global marketing agency. She is also a passionate home cook and blogger whose life and health have been transformed by food. An Instant Pot® evangelist, she loves to share how the appliance has changed the way she cooks for herself and her family, providing ingredient shortcuts and how-to advice for all types of Indian dishes to enjoy streamlined, easy, and delicious recipes for everything from weeknights to family gatherings. Urvashi and her family live in Dallas, Texas.

Connect with Urvashi!
BLOG TwoSleevers.com
PINTEREST pinterest.com/TwoSleevers
FACEBOOK facebook.com/TwoSleever

If you make one of Urvashi's recipes, send pictures and feedback! She answers all questions posted on TwoSleevers.com, as well as on her Facebook page.

CPSIA information can be obtained
at www.ICGtesting.com
Printed in the USA
LVHW01s1609221117
557170LV00001B/1/P